POSTER
IN HISTORY

Below: Bayswater Omnibus, *by William Joy, 1840. Oil on canvas. Publicity posters appear inside the carriage. London, Victoria and Albert Museum.*

the POSTER
IN HISTORY

by Max Gallo

With essays by Carlo Arturo Quintavalle

THE WELLFLEET PRESS
WELLFLEET

WITHDRAWN

Originally published in Italian under the title *I Manifesti*.
Copyright © 1972, © 1989 Arnoldo Mondadori Editore S.p.A., Milan
English translation copyright © 1974 The Hamlyn Publishing Group Limited
and © 1989 Arnoldo Mondadori Editore S.p.A., Milan

Translated by Alfred and Bruni Mayor
Additional material translated by Sara Harris

This 1989 edition published by
The Wellfleet Press
a division of Book Sales, Inc.
110 Enterprise Avenue
Secaucus, NJ 07094

ISBN 1-55521-410-X

Printed and bound in Italy by Arnoldo Mondadori, Verona

Contents

1789 – 1848
From the Bastille to the "Industrial Wonders"   7

1848–1898
The Triumph of the Middle Class   26

1898–1914
The Products of the *Belle Époque*   47

1914–1924
Images of War and Revolution   131

1925–1945
Propaganda and Ideology   158

1950–1970
Words and Images   196

1970–1990
Fragmentation of Society, Uniformity of the Image   217

The Development of Poster Art   238

The Poster: from Political Message to Collector's Item   253

Bibliography   255

BULLETIN

DES AMIS DE LA VÉRITÉ

PUBLIÉ PAR LES DIRECTEURS

DE L'IMPRIMERIE DU CERCLE SOCIAL.

...pectus de ce journal dans ...s, (novembre) rédigée

Une Bouche de Fer, dont les Directeurs ont seuls la clef, est ouverte nuit et jour, rue du Théâtre-François, n° 4, pour tous

les avis et dénonciations ; il en sera fait u... sans compromettre les auteurs qui voudr... rester inconnus.

...e l'abonnement, 18 livres, franc de port pour 3 moi... ...ur l'année.

PARIS,

Chez l... ...rs de l'imprimerie du Cercle Social, rue du Théâtre-François n° 4.

1789–1848
From the Bastille to the "Industrial Wonders"

Less than sixty years elapsed between the French Revolution in 1789 and the revolutions in the rest of Europe, between the time when the theory of the divine right of kings was shaken in Paris to the time when thrones were toppled in Vienna, Milan, Berlin, Prague, Budapest, Rome. But this turbulent half century saw the birth of new political and social ideas whose effects would be felt for generations. In storming the Bastille, a royal fortress in the heart of Paris' working-class district, the French revolutionaries overthrew principles that were centuries old. In place of the ancient system, which had given power to the nobles and the clergy, they adopted the radical Declaration of the Rights of Man and Citizen, proclaimed abstractly but superbly in the phrase "Liberty, equality, fraternity."

From then on, because these words already expressed the intellectual and social expectations of Europe's industrious and cultivated middle class, or bourgeoisie, the contagion spread from country to country, from region to region, from class to class. The concept of liberty, equality, and fraternity would eventually bring about the erosion of the entire existing social and political structure.

Actually, after the initial outbreaks of revolutionary fervor, the law, the militia, and the army were present to see that the abstract principles of liberty, equality, and fraternity in fact favored only the middle class. In addition, Napoleon and later the reinstated monarchs everywhere did their best to stop the contagion, restoring conservative governments that ignored the growing clamor for reforms. Yet during that half century, restraints were everywhere subjected to such pressures that one could foresee their eventual permanent overthrow. Industry and the goods it produced, the growing masses of urban workers and consumers, the birth of the romantic movement, a higher standard of living—all these developments encouraged men to hope for better things and eventually led to the revolutions of 1848.

The changes that began in 1789 were re-flected on city walls. At the time of the French Revolution the walls became animated, alive with posters. Some called for an assembly of citizens, others for an uprising. Posters convoked the sans-culottes (literally, "without breeches," a nickname for the French republicans, who had rejected the breeches worn by the upper class in favor of pantaloons). They invited the citizens to buy the *Bulletin of the Friends of Truth* or the vitriolic journal *Le Père Duchesne*. The cries of street vendors and the words of popular songs and posters reinforced each other. They reflected the revolutionary climate, the political tension, the passion with which groups opposed each other in this period of open class struggle.

Posters proclaimed that traditional notions of everyday behavior were no longer valid because the battle in progress was for "freedom or death," and there could be no "freedom for the enemies of freedom." The posters were crude, the words direct, for in revolutionary times the poster cannot be subtle. It guides or demands; it invites denunciation or participation; it lists suspects; it incites people to hate. In short, it plays an active role in shaping events.

But the poster is also a record of the times. During the events beginning in 1789, the liberty cap, the words "Liberty, equality, fraternity," and the slogan "Long live the Republic" were seen and heard everywhere in the streets. The poster, along with the almanac, conveyed these symbols of the Revolution. It also recorded the events that the revolutionaries considered most important. It showed that in the opinion of the masses the taking of the Tuileries, Louis XVI's residence in Paris, on August 10, 1792, signified the end of an era. A scene from this battle, between contingents of the National Guard, in blue, and the King's Swiss Guard, in red, adorned the almanac of the republic's first year. The poster was a reminder, a memory, an account of events.

With the onset of the Revolution, everyday life became permeated with politics. Newspapers multiplied, spreading their violent opinions and making the citizens more politi-

Poster for the Bulletin des Amis de la Vérité, *1792. Printed in Paris by the Cercle Social. Paris, Musée Carnavalet.*

cally aware. Children played revolution, disguising themselves as sans-culottes or soldiers. The wind of revolution swept all levels of society, creating a new point of view whose premises were that the new order was at one with the order of the universe; that a common reason ruled man and the world; that a Supreme Being presided over the efforts of those seeking to establish the happiness of the human race.

But when this new point of view became the official one, imposed on the country by the revolutionary government rather than spontaneously adopted by the people, it became bombastic. And because discipline is one of the requirements of battle, public spontaneity was controlled, channeled, and soon reduced. For a while in France revolutionary order prevailed effectively; but as Robespierre's lieutenant Louis de Saint-Just pointed out, once victorious, "revolution is frozen."

Further, a coalition of foreign enemies—including every great European power except Russia—began a war with France in 1792. In order to resist this European coalition, as well as a revolt of monarchists and farmers in the Vendée in the west of France, the leaders of the Revolution found it necessary to discipline and supervise the masses, to entrust only a few with power, and thereby to introduce dictatorship for the public good. Once dictatorship existed, however, the meaning of "public good" changed completely. Its definition became the province of officials, of the bureaucrats of the Revolution, the police, and soon the military.

At this point poster art changed too. What had been the fulfillment of a daily need for expression became propaganda. Although attempts to move the viewer were still in evidence, the introduction of conventional imagery made it very clear that a new relationship had been established between the Revolution and the citizen. The Revolution lost its violent and cruel image. Crude words were no longer scrawled on the walls, nor was anyone urged to make denunciations or pursue suspects. Corpses no longer lay on the paving stones of the Tuileries, wreathed in the smoke of battle.

As society again became stable, the Rev-

Paris Newspaper Vendor, 1791. Print made after a water color by Louis Debucourt. Paris, Bibliothèque Nationale.

ALMANACH POUR LA PRESENTE ANNEE

VIVE LA
REPUBLIQUE

olution was exploited. There was formulated a revolutionary myth that survived into the middle of the twentieth century, growing year after year in successive interpretations. The ruined walls of the Bastille, symbol of the old order, rose again on the covers of illustrated magazines. The Bastille, a fixed point of reference in the popular imagination in France, became a degraded symbol, a marketing aid on an advertising poster. The Revolution was assimilated: it was dead. One had only to look in the streets, where the Napoleonic order reigned after Napoleon's accession to power in 1799. Citizens no longer created disturbances or assembled for processions; there was no more public expression of what was called popular emotion. The citizens once again became observers—idlers invited to attend orderly coronation ceremonies or military parades.

Outside France the Revolution doubtless continued to be contagious, because some

FRATERNITÉ
OU LA MORT

SUITE

UNITÉ
DIVISIBILITÉ
DE LA
RÉPUBLIQUE

11

of the principles of 1789 marched with the armies of Napoleon, arousing the people of Italy in 1796–97 and of Germany and Poland in the campaigns of 1805–7. But very soon the warm receptions initially enjoyed by the Grand Army gave way to the general hostility toward an occupying nation. Lampoons and posters berating Napoleon appeared. London was the center of this violent and relentless propaganda, but even in France caricatures and lampoons circulated, some of them on the walls. They show that as the empire grew the popularity of "the monster Bonaparte" decreased. As he continued to make war, Napoleon needed more and more young draftees for his army; in the countryside and in the mountains deserters multiplied. Some young men went so far as to mutilate themselves in order to avoid conscription. Thus an underground opposition to Bonaparte began to grow.

But these events came later in Napoleon's reign. At first in France an apparently obedient, contented population resided in the cities, which the emperor beautified with monuments, trophies, and works of art stolen from the great capitals of Europe. Fed up with revolutionary government and yearning for stability, Frenchmen had welcomed Napoleon. As posters proclaimed, "the immortal Napoleon's" early glory lay not in military victories but in the "peace" he brought. Ironically the conqueror, the maker of war, was popular because he appeared at first as the "messenger of peace."

Not only did Napoleon promise to establish peace on the borders by defeating the anti-French coalition of European kings and emperors, but he also pledged peace within France. These twin promises united all classes and parties. "Neither revolutionary nor aristocrat, I am a nationalist," said Bonaparte. The crowd standing before the poster of "the immortal Napoleon" suggests that new unity.

Napoleon's empire, amalgamating as it did the old order and the conquests of the Revolution, was not a return to the past but a military legitimization of the social order born of the Revolution: the ascendancy of the middle class. In the eyes of his monarchist enemies, Napoleon was a "usurper" of kings, a "Robespierre on horseback." Yet this hatred felt by partisans of the old order was also a factor in Bonaparte's success. He was the rampart against the past, against the disorder of both the monarchy and the Revolution. He maintained stability. After the torment of the Revolution he was the law, and his was a reign of order.

Yet Napoleon's rule maintained the appearance of sovereignty. He revived the cult of personal power. Like a king, he claimed divine right and was crowned by the Pope. He created a new aristocracy, imperial but just as privileged as the old one. Under the empire, society, which had been leveled for a while by a wave of egalitarianism, became again a collection of clearly defined hierarchies. In his effort to establish his own dynasty the emperor borrowed heavily from monarchist etiquette; like a French king, he tried to link himself by marriage with one

Poster for a Grand Bal Paré *(Great costume ball)*, 1810. Printed in Paris by Ogier. Paris, *Musée des Arts Décoratifs.*

of the great reigning families of Europe.

In these ways the empire gave new life to old customs. Assembled around the emperor was an often clumsy court trying to ape Versailles. The nobles who rallied to the empire not only set the tone but provided the examples. In Paris people took up their traditional round of festivities again. After the rattle of the tumbrels that had taken the condemned to the guillotine, after the uncertainty that the Reign of Terror and the denunciations had caused many of the notables, a time of distractions and the Grand Bal Paré (great fancy-dress ball) returned. But there was a difference. While it is true that the imperial eagle presided over the merrymaking, the fancy-dress ball, formerly a prerogative of the aristocracy, was now commercially organized and was open to all for a few francs. Everyone was welcome, and for women the fee was waived. Thus, even though social hierarchies were re-established, even though there was still an aristocracy—both imperial and composed of the old order—the new customs, while inspired by the old, became more democratic.

The differences were noticeable. Society before 1789 was based on classes living according to immutable principles, while the society that grew from the Revolution, and that Napoleon consolidated, was newly middle class—that is to say, it recognized wealth as the prime mover. Naturally money had been a power to reckon with before the storming of the Bastille, but it was not recognized as supreme until after the Revolution. The sun king of the new society was the gold piece. "Get rich," the historian and statesman Francois Guizot would say before long to Louis Philippe's deputies. Money, profit, sales—these characteristic elements of the capitalist system pervaded every aspect of life. Selling was important, **13** and in order to sell products the use of advertisements and posters increased.

The commercial and economic function of the poster became more and more evident. But to sell, one must use reassuring and persuasive symbols. Unlike the bold posters of the Revolution, with their direct language and crude words, the commercial posters of the empire used symbols to encourage potential buyers to make certain favorable associations. For instance, in order to sell "a good double-strength beer," one poster showed beer being bought by soldiers of the imperial guard, whose weapons, hats, and glittering uniforms symbolized glory as well as physical and military strength. Beer seems appropriate to this martial setting of parades and armed men.

The Bourbon monarchy was restored in 1814, and after a few years Louis XVIII began acceding to ultraroyalist demands to reinstate the old order. But the structure and principles of society had been modified so much that any attempt to revive privilege and a prerevolutionary fixed hierarchy was doomed to failure. The idea of ownership of the earth by the middle class, the idea of equality based on wealth, in short the idea of money as the decisive criterion was so strong that Charles X, successor to Louis XVIII, was forced to abdicate in 1830 because his monarchy could not be shaped to the social realities.

The new reality was made clear on the posters showing royalty and the reinstated nobility dignifying a tobacco shop just as the imperial grenadiers had dignified beer a few years earlier; while ghosts from the Middle Ages, Death and his scythe, and the gods of the ancient world were used to advertise a public entertainment. Stendhal wrote: "The bank is at the head of the state. The middle class has replaced the aristocracy, and the bank is the nobility of the middle class."

Within the middle class, distinctions based on wealth were just as marked as those that had separated various grades of the nobility under the old order. In a single French provincial city of 1840, one could distinguish eight different social groups, from those who enjoyed an income of twelve thousand francs, owned carriages and stables, employed coachmen, and spent

Débit de Tabac, Manufacture Royale *(Tobacco shop, royal monopoly), about 1820. The style is similar to that of the poster* Bonne Double Bière. *Paris, private collection.*

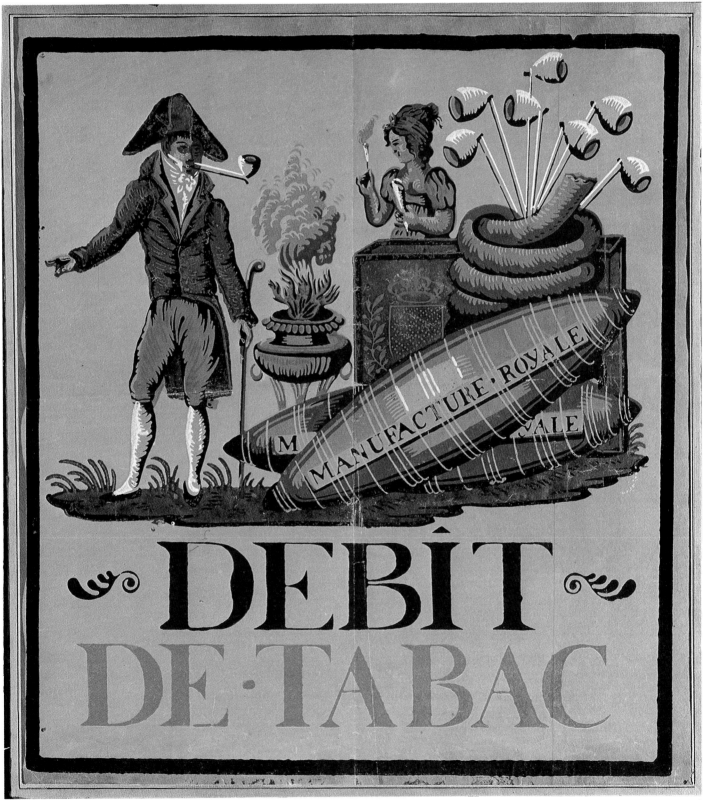

Taxed No More!!! *Anonymous English poster, about 1830. London, Library of London University.*

part of the year at a spa or at the seaside, to those who subsisted on an annual income of only two thousand francs. Despite a tendency toward uniformity (no one wore wigs anymore), a person's appearance often indicated the size of his fortune. One could hardly mistake the workman in his smock and cap for the bourgeois in his frock coat and top hat; and the differences in the way women dressed were even more marked.

A society founded on money is hard on women. Excluded from working, middle-class women were forced to rely on their fortune or their beauty, two attributes of equal importance. The dowry was at the core of all middle-class marriages and caused many tragedies; but because of it a girl could marry and achieve material security and moral satisfaction. Beauty, although transitory, was the wealth of those without fortune, and because it was a form of merchandise, it was manufactured.

Posters advertising the openings of beauty shops multiplied. There were "depilatory salons," where the wear and tear of age was fought, where gray hair "which would lower a woman's value" was removed. Other posters advertised flattering, form-fitting dresses, decorated with lace and ribbons and shown in bright colors, with low-cut necklines that revealed the shoulders.

Because of the attention that more and more women gave to their appearance, the retail sales of beauty products and of fashionable knickknacks increased greatly, especially as their use spread to the lower middle classes. In this sense the posters advertising beauty products or attractive shops were indicative of a certain democratization of customs, although the benefits had not yet reached the growing working class or the peasantry. In fact workers and peasants were not yet a part of the audience to which posters were addressed.

The idlers who gathered in the street in front of the "pictures of everyday life" were virtually without exception members of the middle class, recognizable by their frock coats and top hats. There were a few women, but the majority of strollers were men, because the middle-class woman still was allowed into the street only on special occasions. Moreover, despite the police, the streets were dangerous. The flight from the country, the shift in population, and the appeal of growing industries brought unruly masses to the cities. These people settled on the outskirts, victims of poverty and epidemics like the cholera epidemic that swept Europe between 1830 and 1835. Certain vaguely defined areas were veritable jungles where law enforcement was known to be negligible.

The middle class lived in fear of what critic François Saint-Marc Girardin called the "barbarians in the suburbs of our industrial cities." To protect themselves, burghers everywhere considered forming national guards, and they appealed to their countries' armies because the police forces were insufficient. But because the workers' misery was real and their mortality rate inhuman,

L'Homme-Affiche du Boulevard du Temple *(The sandwich man of the Boulevard du Temple), about 1820. Anonymous water color. Paris, Musée Carnavalet.*

Distraction d'un Afficheur *(Amusement of a billsticker), about 1820. Anonymous colored engraving. Paris, Musée Carnavalet.*

insurrection could not effectively be prevented. Between 1830 and 1848 the cities and villages of Europe were shaken by rebellions that, like those of the silk weavers of Lyons in 1831 and 1834, were in fact rebellions against hunger. "To live working or to die fighting" and "Bread or lead" were the silk weavers' slogans. Workers rose in Piedmont, Lombardy, Venetia, Flanders, England, and Paris.

These short, violent, and disorganized insurrections were everywhere put down. "There is no need for mercy," wrote statesman and historian Adolphe Thiers. But the horror, the barbarism, the violence, and the inequality remained. Beneath the apparent stability of a privileged class, millions of people lived a sordid existence.

There were two worlds, separated by habits, dress, and points of view. The middle class was already disciplined. In the other world men were rough, oppressed. To the middle class the man from the other world was only merchandise, fit to carry sandwich boards like a mobile wall. Wearing a smock and an enormous hat or cap, the poster man was dressed to look ridiculous so that idlers would stop and look at his posters. The poster man was a symbol of an era in which the common man was considered of little worth.

Education made some difference. But the ability to read spread very slowly, despite the large number of publications available. First there were the tabloid newspapers. In 1836 in Paris, Émile de Girardin started *La Presse*, a daily containing advertisements, official notices, stock-exchange quotations, and a market report. Other cities also had their tabloids. The press agencies (Havas in 1835, Reuters, and others) provided the news, advertisers paid for space, and the first

rotating mechanical presses made rapid printing possible. The tabloids were obviously read by the well-to-do, but they also reached the lower middle class and the artisans. They created public opinion, widened horizons, and spread political policy. The press also helped develop a new national awareness, which from the 1840's onward began to manifest itself from Milan to Prague, from Palermo to Berlin.

In addition, newspapers published novels in daily installments. In Paris readers bought a paper for the continuation of a story by Pierre Alexis Ponson du Terrail or Honoré de Balzac. (Balzac nonetheless wrote that "all the newspapers are despicable, hypocritical, infamous, liars, murderers . . . they kill ideas, systems, people, and flourish because they do so.") Bold posters advertised the newspaper serials. These posters reached the broadest possible audience, cutting across class lines to catch the eye of all Paris.

Newspapers and the illustrated serials were passed from reader to reader because they were still too expensive for everyone to buy. And as the number of readers grew, the serial became a means of influencing the opinions of a mass audience. With the help of these serials, for instance, the Napoleonic legend was spread through all levels of society. It was easy to imagine that the tales were the recollections of an old soldier remembering past glories during a night watch. In reality, hack writers created the legends of the "Little Corporal," the "Veteran of the Imperial Guard," and the lady canteenkeeper. By means of these legends, the public attitude toward the Napoleonic era was manipulated: Napoleon was portrayed as the father of soldiers and the people, the defender of revolutionary ideals, the messenger of peace who had to fight the threat of monarchist conspiracies. Many tears were shed for this romantic hero who knew glory and died in exile.

If Napoleon's image was so popular, if he seemed to be a republican monarch, and if that contradiction in terms did not shock the people, it was because in post-Napoleonic

Left: interior poster for Le Diamant du Commandeur, a serial by Pierre Alexis Ponson du Terrail. Signed "Belloguet" at lower left, about 1845. Printed in Paris by Proust. Paris, Musée des Arts Décoratifs.

Center: interior poster for La Jeunesse du Roi Henri, by Ponson du Terrail. Signed "Belloguet" at lower right, about 1845. Printed in Paris by Proust. A detail appears below. Paris, Musée des Arts Décoratifs.

Below: interior poster in black and white for Comment Meurent les Femmes (How women die), by Carle Ledhuy. Signed "Adolphe Lalance Barbouillavit" at lower left. Not dated, about 1840. Paris, Musée des Arts Décoratifs.

France and in the rest of Europe rigid, conservative, often repressive governments and such restrictive diplomatic systems as the Holy Alliance made the Napoleonic era appear in retrospect to be one of youthfulness and national emancipation. A growing popular dissatisfaction throughout Europe was threatening the system that had been established by Austria's reactionary Minister of Foreign Affairs, Prince Klemens von Metternich, at the Congress of Vienna in 1815.

Tension mounted until finally, in 1848, revolutions erupted across Europe. Italy was shaken with nationalist tremors, as were central Europe and Germany. Austria was struck squarely, because if the revolution was to spread and prevail, the keystone of the system, Vienna, had to crumble. All over Europe, in all languages, the cries "Long live liberty" and "Long live independence" could be heard. Prorevolutionary newspapers proclaimed the establishment of revolutionary governments. Nationalists scrawled slogans on the walls. As in 1789, words were a weapon in the hands of the revolutionaries.

But has the power of words ever been sufficient? By the end of 1848, all across Europe, order was being restored as liberals and patriots in country after country were defeated. In Paris the "barbarians" were forced back into their districts. Austrian armies subdued the Czech, Hungarian, and Italian nationalists. Finally the Germans had to give way. There were no more re-

Poster for Petites Misères de la Vie Conjugale *(Small miseries of married life), by Honoré de Balzac. Published in fifty installments, with three hundred drawings by Bertall. Dated 1845. Paris, Bibliothèque Nationale.*

sounding words, no more spontaneous proclamations on the walls. After the violence and the executions in the streets, after the fear that the well-to-do classes had felt before the popular uprising, life had once more become secure, subject only to the risks of bad luck and destiny. Advertisements replaced proclamations on the walls. One poster advertising insurance used glorious, virile symbols—flags, cocks, and bolts of lightning—and military language. Order seemed assured; people could have confidence in the future.

There was a rapid rebirth of public confidence, because technical and scientific advances seemed to those who benefited from them to guarantee an expansion of knowledge and profits. People believed in the growth of industry. Since the beginning of the nineteenth century, new inventions such as the steam engine and the loom had revolutionized industrial production. It was the beginning of the era of metallurgy, of rapid communications (Samuel F. B. Morse's first telegraph line was installed in the United States in 1844), of the railroad (George Stephenson's first steam engine was patented in England in 1815), of mass production. The geography of industrial Europe changed, regions began to specialize (the Ruhr and the Creusot areas, for instance, became important mining centers), landscapes were transformed, and people began to flock to the mines and to the industrial cities.

Industrialization contained the seeds of its own expansion: the extension of the railroad system (in 1848 there were 1,206 miles of track in France, 3,750 miles in England) stimulated the iron and steel industry; the latter consumed ever greater quantities of coal. The different branches of production were interrelated, and the new techniques brought society into the industrial era.

It was a time of utopian schemes that embodied the hopes raised by scientific and technical developments. The utopians sought to satisfy the need for brotherhood, organization, and justice—a need that grew out of crying social inequities and econ-

Interior poster for La Porteuse de Pain *(The bread vendor), by Xavier de Montépin. Neither signed nor dated, about 1850. Printed by Delanchy-Ancourt. Paris, Musée des Arts Décoratifs.*

Interior poster for the Histoire de la Garde Impériale *(Story of the imperial guard), by Marco de Saint-Hilaire, in fifty installments. Neither signed nor dated, about 1850. Paris, Musée des Arts Décoratifs.*

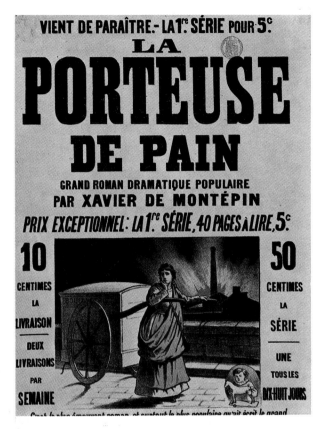

omic crises. Many of these schemes reflected a new ideology, socialism (the word appeared in Italy in 1803, in England in 1822, and in France in 1831), which, broadly, advocated that private property should disappear and that labor should appropriate the wealth it produced.

The Comte de Saint-Simon (1760–1825) preached a reorganization of society in which scholars, engineers, and other talented men would possess power. Among the works in which he presented his doctrine were *Reorganization of European Society* (1814) and *Industrialists' Catechism* (1823–24). "France," he wrote, "has become a large factory and the French nation a large workshop. This factory should be run like other factories." Around Saint-Simon were gathered young scholars, philosophers, and engineers who believed in the idea of rapid industrial development. They were the originators of many great engineering works—the Suez Canal, for example—and other innovations that left their mark on the nineteenth century. Another social reformer, Charles Fourier, in *The New Industrial World* (1829–30) argued for an era of complete harmony in which people would live in largely agricultural communes, which he called *phalanstères* (from *phalange*, meaning "phalanx," and *monastère*, meaning "monastery").

These and other utopian schemes suggest that despite technical successes and the rise in production, many felt that an equilibrium among men and among classes of men had not yet been achieved. Remedies were sought in utopias and in other new schemes for economic and political organization. The very foundations of society were questioned. In 1840 the social reformer Pierre Joseph Proudhon asked himself, "What is property?" and answered, "Property is theft." In the *Communist Manifesto* of January, 1848, Karl Marx wrote: "For some decades the history of industry and com-

23

merce has been none other than the history of the revolt of the modern productive force against the modern regime of production, against a form of ownership on which the existence of the middle class is based." And he issued his famous plea: "Workers of the world, unite."

However, it was not this slogan that animated the revolutionaries of 1848. Too many differences separated the cities from the countryside, region from region within each nation, and the east and south of Europe from the partially industrialized west. The insurgents of 1848 were moved by different motives—some by demands for equality, others by nationalism. It was these motives that inspired simultaneous revolts by Parisians, Czechs, Milanese, and Berliners.

Another reason the workers did not rally to Marx's battle cry in 1848 was that they were still very much a minority. Nevertheless, the unsuccessful uprisings of 1848 helped them discover their strengths and weaknesses and made them realize that they formed a coherent group. They discovered that they had their own goals and could choose their own leaders without following the politicians of the middle or lower middle classes. For the first time in history they participated in government when a French worker by the name of Albert was made part of the provisional government of the February revolution. This government decreed the right to work and created national workshops. In this way, February, 1848, revealed the power of the proletariat to the workers themselves.

But it was only a brief ray of light. Most often—as the poster announcing an 1844 industrial exposition shows—the workers were lost in a crowd of stylish folk. The artist showed only a few workers wielding a hammer on an anvil or pulling an ancient locomotive. And at the exhibitions organized by the industries to which they were indispensable, they appeared only as shadows. It was as if society were ashamed to admit that it was possible to show these industrial wonders only because of the pain, misery, and misfortune of the common man.

24

Title page of a Milan daily paper proclaiming March 22, 1848, as the first day of independence in Lombardy. Milan, State Archives.

LES PRODIGES
de **L'INDUSTRIE**

EXPOSITION DE 1844,

Par Louis Huart . 80 vignettes par Cham,
Daumier, Maurisset

PRIX 1 Fr.

Imp. d'Aubert & Cie

1848–1898
The Triumph
of the Middle Class

From 1848 to the end of the nineteenth century a metamorphosis took place in Europe and in the world. What had begun to take shape during the first half of the century in a few privileged regions was developed fully in the majority of countries. The railroad, for instance, which at first had been used to link coal-mining towns within a relatively small area, now crossed the entire North American continent from coast to coast. The sea trip between Europe and the Far East was more than cut in half with the opening of the Suez Canal in 1869. The age of the machine, of iron and steel, of banks, railroads, and cities gave the world a new rhythm. The days and lives of millions of people were measured and regulated by schedules of industrial production.

In these fifty years the map of Europe and the world changed profoundly. Europe became so powerful that it looked beyond its boundaries to new territories and established vast colonial empires. The division of Africa and Asia, barely outlined in 1848, was an accomplished fact fifty years later. One reason behind the push into new territories was that Europe was bursting with manufactured products for which both raw materials and outlets were needed. But above all the population exploded, growing from 266 million to 401 million between 1850 and 1900. As a result, millions of Europeans emigrated, penetrating the most distant countries. Italians, Germans, Englishmen, Poles, and Irishmen crossed the oceans, impelled by poverty and attracted by the hope of making their fortune or simply of surviving in a new land. Even a rise in Europe's standard of living and significant political changes could not check this exodus. In the United States, the frontier had by 1890 reached the Pacific Coast.

In Europe the nationalist movements, which had been frustrated in 1848, overcame all resistance. By 1871 Italy had achieved a national identity, and the German states were unified following their victory over France in the war of 1870–71. But the conquering of new lands and the drawing of new frontiers did not insure

Poster advertising industrial apartment houses in the Faubourg St. Antoine in Paris. About 1870–75. Printed by F. Appel. Paris, Musée des Arts Décoratifs.

DIX-NEUF IMMEUBLES CONFORTABLES

SERVICE DE CONCIERGES

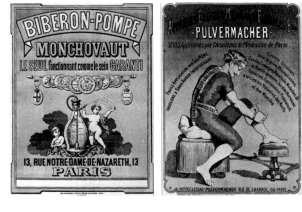

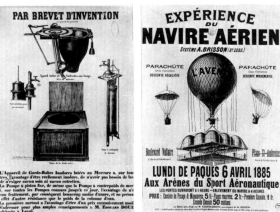

peace. True, the second half of the nineteenth century—despite the Civil War in the United States, the Crimean War, and the Franco-Prussian War—seemed remarkably peaceful compared to the first half or to the twentieth century. But the seeds of future conflict were already being sown on the eve of what has been wrongly called the *belle époque.*

The inequalities that had set classes and social groups against one another in the first half of the century persisted. Society was still cruel to its poorest members; but the proletariat, or working class, had grown in numbers and strength, and all industrial cities were subjected to clashes between bands of workmen and the police or military. Strikes proliferated and were severely repressed. Socialist parties organized, but governments resisted them.

In some states universal suffrage gave at least the appearance of a consensus. In 1851 in France, for instance, it led to a plebiscite that allowed Napoleon III to seize power. But popularly elected governments could not prevent the gravest conflicts: the Paris Commune of 1871, the bloodiest of all nineteenth-century insurrections, was a rebellion by the people of Paris against the government of France after the country at large had supported a peace treaty with Germany.

The profound causes of these conflicts can be traced to working conditions and the state of industrial development. Despite the standardization of production techniques—the result of growing numbers of factories and the widespread use of machines—the individual craftsman still survived in all countries. Indeed, cottage industry was on the increase, at least partly as a result of the invention of machines that were easy to carry and install (the sewing machine, for example). In these home industries—which concentrated on the production of dresses, lingerie, leather goods, furniture, and shoes—the workers, including large numbers of women, were greatly exploited. They were entirely dependent on the manufacturer to advance them money to rent or

Poster advertising the various wares of an iron foundry called the Carré Factory. Neither signed nor dated, about 1870. Printed in Paris by Jules Chéret. Paris, Musée des Arts Décoratifs.

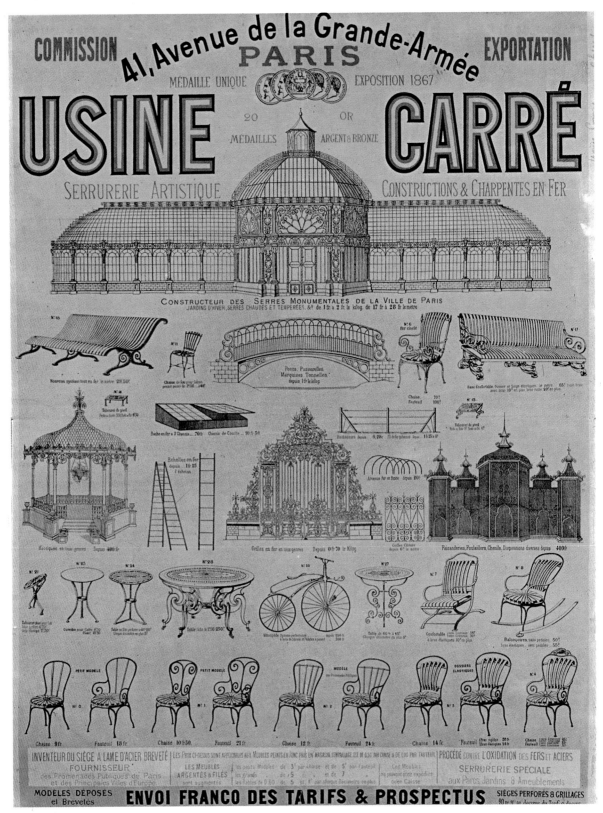

buy the machine that was then installed in their home. They also depended on him to give them work and raw materials as well as to sell the finished product.

In certain quarters of the big cities—such as the eastern part of Paris, the Faubourg St. Antoine—workers lived in buildings that contained both their working and living quarters, continuing a practice that had been common among artisans in the sixteenth and seventeenth centuries. During urban uprisings—the Commune, for example—the quarters that became strongholds of insurrection were those where the rebels were also resident workers. One reason was that those artisans working at home were the first to be affected by fluctuating market conditions. The development of the capitalist system was far from orderly: financial crises occurred every decade (1847, 1857, 1866, 1873, 1882, 1890). The resulting unemployment provoked a rapid decline in consumption, and the first to be

affected were individual workers who produced goods for sale to a middleman, or those artisans who depended directly on the marketplace.

Furthermore, these economic crises resulted in price fluctuations of long duration. Thus, between 1873 and 1895 there was a serious depression, during which prices and salaries sank. To compensate for the decline, new techniques were developed to lower production costs and increase production. But in those difficult times competition was cutthroat, and the weakest—those who could not afford to buy improved machinery or wait for a time of higher prices—disappeared. The situation favored the largest enterprises and accelerated the process of industrial concentration and specialization.

The concern over sales led industries to expand their areas of operation. Artisans once more faced the kind of competition that could only wipe them out. Some factories were retailing their own products. They published brochures and catalogues advertising the sale of everything from ironwork for large construction projects to armchairs, tables, and locks. Their range of products was enormous, and they lowered their prices until their competitors were ruined.

Particularly in the iron industry, factories proliferated. The production of goods made from iron required large investments, powerful machinery, links with the mining industry, and constant dealings with banks. All this was possible only for large-scale capitalism, which as a result took over the iron and coal industries, the two decisive industries during the second half of the nineteenth century.

The age of iron really began after 1850. At the production level, the techniques of Henry Bessemer, William Siemens, Sidney Thomas, Percy Gilchrist, and Pierre Martin made possible the construction of converters and furnaces that produced a better steel with predictable properties. Steel became the material of the century. It replaced wood or leather in everything from large

engineering projects to chairs, from arch supports in boots and reinforcements in shoe soles to bicycles. Huge engineering feats, the symbols of the century, were made of steel: the Eiffel Tower, the Brooklyn Bridge, the bridge over the Firth of Forth, the skeletons that supported the glass-covered galleries of Milan and Paris. Steel was everywhere changing daily life.

Another industry, the chemical industry, made its appearance during this half century. Although less developed than metallurgy, it also altered daily living. It contributed to increased agricultural production with fertilizers and insecticides. It altered the fashion industry with new dyes for fabrics. Matches gave everyone access to fire; gas lighting spread. Soaps and new medicines contributed to cleanliness and better health care, new habits that helped increase life expectancy. Advertising posters showed people taking care of their teeth and hair, letting specialists supervise the birth of their children. Thanks to advances in technology and urbanization, old practices were being abandoned. Slowly a new civilization was emerging.

This new civilization had its temples. The first of these were devoted to entertainment, for as society became urban, it also became more secular. In the yellow gaslight, people gathered to dance to Strauss waltzes and to polkas and mazurkas, or to listen to the music of Jacques Offenbach. Operas and operettas attracted great crowds. The opera house—with its luxurious interiors, bril-

AUX VIOLETTES

DEUIL COMPLET TOUT FAIT OU SUR MESURE en 8 heures

80, Rue de Clichy

This poster offers complete mourning outfits custom made within eight hours at a shop called Aux Violettes. Not signed, about 1880. Printed in Paris by H. Laas. Paris, Musée des Arts Décoratifs.

liantly lighted chandeliers, and rich voices— was an island in the city, where a venerable tradition of song and spectacle was preserved. The most popular art form of the nineteenth century, opera was a refuge, an escape. Charles Gounod's *Faust* and the operas of Richard Wagner and Giuseppe Verdi, sumptuous and passionate, rejected the reality of the city, of industry. They returned to legend.

All this took place in a society in which science, industry, and technology played increasingly important roles. Their products were on display in the other great urban temple: the department store. With their long elevated galleries, their columns, tapestries, sculptures, and chandeliers, department stores greatly resembled opera houses. They too were a feast for the eye, an invitation to dream, a stimulus to the emotions. Each department store was a complete shopping street. For the small shops that had remained unchanged since the beginning of the century, the arrival of these "selling factories" was ruinous. In the department stores one could find, for example, an entire trousseau in a short time, in a single luxurious place, and for low prices. The small shops could not compete. And unlike department stores, small businesses did not have the means to undertake extensive advertising.

The posters and announcements of the department stores captivated everyone, playing on the obscure motivations that make people buy things. The dress-shop poster that shows an engaging young widow holding a bunch of violets was obviously designed to attract customers by suggesting elegance and seduction, not tragedy. The

33

poster seems to say that new happiness is possible, that widowhood passes in an instant, that a change in fashion opens up a new future; to achieve all this, a widow needed only rely on those who could produce widow's weeds to measure in just eight hours.

Apart from its immediate goal—to sell widow's clothes—this advertising poster also reflected new social attitudes, such as the rejection of religious habits, the loosening of Catholicism's hold over women, and women's growing lack of submissiveness. It was no longer scandalous to be a "merry

OVERLEAF: *poster for Crespin & Dufayel, one of the largest Paris department stores. The words on the glass dome read: ''Fixed prices marked in plain figures.'' Not signed, about 1880–85. Printed in Paris by H. Laas. Paris, Musée des Arts Décoratifs.*

Poster and detail (below) for a large Paris department store, Au Moine Saint-Martin, about 1875. Paris, Musée des Arts Décoratifs.

widow.'' Advertising in this case both mirrored a state of mind and involuntarily but efficiently disseminated that state of mind.

In this poster and others issued by department stores, the models were clearly members of the middle class. Their status was apparent in their clothing: men, women, and children were dressed according to middle-class tastes. It was also apparent in the typical middle-class attitude toward children. Boys and girls were small reproductions of their fathers and mothers. Modeled in the image of their parents, they were expected in turn to produce children just

Ho! For the Gold Mines! An 1865 poster announcing the weekly departures of steamers from St. Louis for the gold-mining district. New York, New-York Historical Society.

Opposite: poster advertising bicycles and tricycles. Neither signed nor dated, probably about 1880. Printed in Paris by F. Appel. Paris, Musée des Arts Décoratifs.

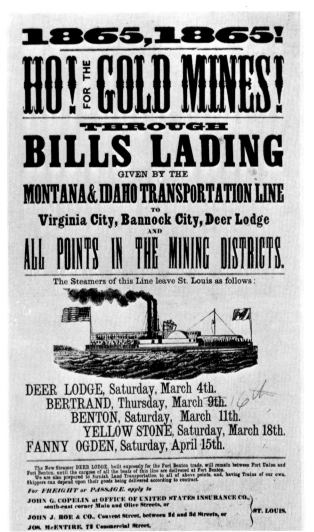

like themselves. In the constantly changing society of the nineteenth century, the ideal affirmed by advertising was stability.

The adoption of middle-class standards by advertising was particularly significant because advertising had taken over the streets and invaded the newspapers. At the end of the century, in France, almost 100 million francs were spent for advertising, of which 40 million went for newspaper advertisements alone. The Crespin & Dufayel department store advertised its vast galleries on huge posters. Thomas Holloway spent more than $500,000 to advertise his miraculous pills. In 1889 a German priest claimed to have received 13,577 printed advertising leaflets.

As city dwellers began to feel beleaguered by the call to buy and by the increasingly fast pace of city life, they felt the need to get away from the pressure. As a result, the tourist movement to seaside resorts or the mountains began. And as daily life became less physically demanding, people began to be preoccupied with keeping up their physical appearance; exercises to give "health, strength, and courage" became popular.

Most important, cities continued to expand enormously. In a hundred years the cities of Europe grew by more than 300 per cent. In 1880 4 million of England's 30 million inhabitants lived in London, and

Advertising poster for beach shoes "patented in France and abroad." Neither signed nor dated, probably about 1880. Printed in Paris by Guillet et Mionllet. Paris, Musée des Arts Décoratifs.

Detail of a poster advertising courses in dancing, fencing, calisthenics for men and women. Neither signed nor dated, about 1880. Printed in Paris by Émile Lévy. Paris, Musée des Arts Décoratifs.

3 million of France's 37 million lived in Paris. An urban way of life evolved on the busy, gaslighted streets. The first bicycles appeared. New streets were cut into the heart of the old quarters; in Paris great boulevards knifed through the historic center. With its diverse activities, cosmopolitan crowds, heavy traffic, vices, and entertainments, the city was the symbol of the second half of the nineteenth century.

All the feverish activity in Western Europe, the changes in society, can be understood by relating the growth of the economy to the increase in available capital, for industrial development had to be financed. Banks installed a network of branches that collected people's savings. The credit system was perfected, and the check became commonplace.

Of great importance was the discovery of new gold mines. Between 1850 and 1870 the supply of gold increased at the same rate that it had between 1500 and 1850. Several times in the century the world was infected by gold fever. In the United States shipping companies advertised "Ho! For the gold mines" and scheduled departures for Colorado, Alaska, and the Klondike. At mine sites, whole towns were constructed. Australia and Africa also attracted prospectors for gold. During the second half of the century there was a real abundance of gold as well as silver.

The United States continued to appear to many poverty-stricken European emigrants as the land of freedom and opportunity. One popular poster, showing a woman waving The Stars and Stripes, symbolized the determination of Northerners to maintain unity and freedom and to insure equality for all, black as well as white. In fact, the image of a woman holding a flag became on both sides of the Atlantic a symbol of the struggle for freedom and the republic. Artists chose woman, presented as mother, wife, and goddess, to symbolize an ideal for a popular audience.

Yet despite this idealization, women remained second-class citizens with limited rights. Of course they fought for equality. During times of revolutionary upheaval—the revolution of 1848 or the Paris Commune, for instance—posters in Paris posed fundamental questions. As one poster asked, "Will women enjoy political and social rights and will they be recognized as men's equals?" Other posters demanded divorce. The socialist movements of the 1880's made women the theoretical equal of men. Yet in one election, in 1885, the "feminist and socialist" candidate could not even get her candidacy registered.

The emancipation of women was opposed not only by existing laws and religious dogma but very often by working-class men. On one subject, divorce, their opposition was at least partly based on economics. A poster that appeared on the walls of Paris expressed the workers' viewpoint: "Divorce? Do workers marry provisionally? A workman takes a wife to live, suffer, and die with her. He does not cast her away when he has had enough of her. And the worker's wife does not want to pass from hand to hand. Furthermore, even if the worker wanted to take advantage of divorce, could he? Could he pay the lawyers and the court fees? Do you know who is asking for divorce? A coalition of advantage and vice. For the rich man, divorce is the right to commit adultery purchased with money; for the rich woman, it is privileged prostitution."

For the socialists in particular, divorce was a menace to the poorest and to women. It would be acceptable only in a different society, where women would earn salaries and where want and poverty would no longer be problems.

Need and poverty diminished during the second half of the century. Health improved, longevity increased. About 1850 the annual mortality rate in Europe was 30 per 1,000; during the last decade in the century it dropped to 26. Great epidemics struck less frequently, and after 1850 food shortages were confined to certain regions in the south and east of Europe. The advent of transatlantic shipping and the cultivation of wheat in Canada and the United States meant that grain could be brought to Europe cheaply.

Conditions were still hard for workers: almost all their earnings were spent on food and rent. They had meat only once a week, and then only the cheap cuts. The working day almost always exceeded twelve hours. Children began to work at the age of ten. Unemployment, sickness, and old age were the greatest worries for the working man.

At the same time, wealth and affluence spread among the privileged few. In England 5 per cent of the inhabitants owned half the property and employed more than a million servants. It is understandable that under these circumstances workers' protests became violent.

After a long quiescence that followed the failure of the June, 1848, insurrection in France, the workers' movement was reborn all over Europe. At first the movement concentrated on improving the material conditions of the proletariat without getting involved in party politics. But once it became apparent that economic claims had political consequences, workers began to organize politically. In 1864 Marx helped found the International Workingmen's Association (known as the First International), whose purpose was to prepare the proletariat for the collapse of capitalism. The labor movement in Germany was the first to become successfully involved in national politics:

the Social Democratic party, formed in Germany in 1869, won 12 seats in the 1877 national elections. Strong workers' organizations sprang up in England. By the 1890's there were socialist parties in most European countries. As a result, the political awareness of the growing working class heightened.

In France during the last years of the reign of Napoleon III, there were a number of particularly violent strikes, many of which included clashes with the army. But the most violent outbreak of all, the establishment of the Paris Commune, followed the destruction of the Second Empire in the Franco-Prussian War.

In January, 1871, France elected a National Assembly that favored peace with Germany. The people of Paris, however, having just endured a long siege, regarded peace as a humiliating capitulation. In March, 1871, they rebelled against the national government at Versailles and set up a communal government. Once more the walls of Paris were covered with proclamations, with words echoing those of 1793 and 1848. The Communards wanted both political reforms (they wanted communes to replace the state as the primary unit of government) and economic reforms. The ensuing fight was violent, passionate, even savage, and it left no room for compromise or conciliation.

The legitimate government at Versailles sent troops to quell the rebellion. While these troops were besieging the city, the Commune came under the control of extremists. Hostages—prominent citizens and clergymen—were killed, public buildings destroyed. After the troops entered the city, they launched their own orgy of slaughter in reprisal. During so-called Bloody Week (May 21–28, 1871), they killed more than fifteen thousand Parisians.

While it left a legacy that still affects French politics, the pitiless repression of the left by the right did not manage to stamp out the workers' movement. On the contrary, the Commune, like the Revolution of 1789, became a legend and as such a milestone. Marx saw it as the first effort at proletarian dictatorship. And in France the cruelty of the Versailles troops persuaded a part of the workers' movement there that only force could bring about the victory of socialism. In Germany and England negotiation and reform were still believed to be more effective means. Slowly but surely, however, the ideas of Marx were everywhere winning adherents in the trade unions and in the workers' parties.

In 1889 in Paris, while a world's fair was presenting the latest discoveries of science and industry, the Second International Congress met, bringing together the socialist parties of Europe. With the Marxists in the majority, it was decided to make the first of May a day of international workers' demonstrations, "so that in all countries and all cities the workers give formal notice to the public authorities that their working day

COMMUNE DE PARIS

Citoyens,

Votre Commune est constituée.

Le vote du **26** mars a sanctionné la Révolution victorieuse.

Un pouvoir lâchement agresseur vous avait pris à la gorge : vous avez, dans votre légitime défense, repoussé de vos murs ce gouvernement qui voulait vous déshonorer en vous imposant un roi.

Aujourd'hui, les criminels que vous n'avez même pas voulu poursuivre abusent de votre magnanimité pour organiser aux portes même de la cité un foyer de conspiration monarchique. Ils invoquent la guerre civile; ils mettent en œuvre toutes les corruptions; ils acceptent toutes les complicités: ils ont osé mendier jusqu'à l'appui de l'étranger.

Nous en appelons de ces menées exécrables au jugement de la France et du monde.

Citoyens,

Vous venez de vous donner des institutions qui défient toutes les tentatives.

Vous êtes maîtres de vos destinées. Forte de votre appui, la représentation que vous venez d'établir va réparer les désastres causés par le pouvoir déchu : l'industrie compromise, le travail suspendu, les transactions commerciales paralysées, vont recevoir une impulsion vigoureuse.

Dès aujourd'hui, la décision attendue sur les loyers;

Demain, celle des échéances;

Tous les services publics rétablis et simplifiés;

La garde nationale, désormais seule force armée de la cité, réorganisée sans délai.

Tels seront nos premiers actes.

Les élus du Peuple ne lui demandent, pour assurer le triomphe de la République, que de les soutenir de sa confiance.

Quant à eux, ils feront leur devoir.

Hôtel-de-Ville de Paris, le 29 mars 1871.

LA COMMUNE DE PARIS.

IMPRIMERIE NATIONALE — Mars 1871.

Opposite: unsigned poster advertising the magazine Le Revanche (Revenge), about 1880. Printed in Paris by Émile Lévy. Paris, Musée des Arts Décoratifs.

Poster advertising Conty guides to the 1878 world's fair. Signed at lower right "Viez." Printed in Paris by F. Appel. Paris, Musée des Arts Décoratifs.

should be legally reduced to eight hours.''

Protest against the established order also took other forms, especially when open activities were repressed. Following a congress of anarchists in London in 1881, individual acts of violence—''propaganda by deed'' as the anarchists called it—increased. Italians, Spaniards, Irishmen, and Frenchmen became the most active disciples of the principal theorist of anarchy, Mikhail Bakunin. The deeds they committed in the name of anarchism made it clear that they no longer believed science and technology would insure social progress. For the anarchist, idealism had been transformed into a violent negation of an unjust society.

This violence affected not only the relationship between the classes but as the century neared its end, international relations as well. In the course of the century, the principle of separate nations had triumphed throughout most of Europe. Only the Austro-Hungarian Empire was still founded on dynastic principles.

Within Europe's new borders, nationalistic feelings flared up. There was much to encourage the trend: the expanding tabloid press stressed nationalist themes—in France, for example, it exploited the theme of revenge after the defeat of 1870; schools glorified the history of the fatherland; compulsory military service brought private citizens into the army, which until then had been made up of professional soldiers. Economic difficulties caused by international competition, the clashes among imperial powers seeking to divide up the world, and colonial ventures all helped to encourage nationalism. Increasingly the statesmen who shaped international relations were forced to take into account the opinion of the urban masses.

This situation was the more dangerous because weapons had been so improved that conflicts were becoming more destructive. Unfortunately not enough people seemed to be concerned. Those who attempted to create an international code of ethics or to set up international peace-keeping institutions were only partially

successful. They failed to achieve a stable peace; the best they could do was to try to make war more humane by means of the Geneva Convention (1864) and the Conference of Saint Petersburg (1868), which forbade the use of explosive bullets.

Meanwhile in the popular imagination war remained glorious and the soldier a hero, and this attitude was reinforced by those who shaped popular opinion. At the end of the nineteenth century, when industry already could produce everything necessary for a modern war, a poster advertising the magazine *Revenge* was presenting an image of war that was archaic and mythical, evoking a glorious, legendary epic.

Even with regard to war, the poster was an advertisement intended to seduce the viewer and make him dream. The reality would prove a cruel surprise.

Poster by Henri de Toulouse-Lautrec advertising the serialized publication in Le Matin of the Abbé Faure's memoirs of confessions he had heard at the foot of the guillotine, 1893. Paris, Musée des Arts Décoratifs.

1898–1914
The Products of the *Belle Époque*

Violence was the persistent undercurrent in the decade and a half before World War I, years that in spirit were still so much a part of the nineteenth century.

At the Moulin Rouge, Paris' best-known nightclub, the frenzied music of the cancan captivated diners. But the swishing of lace and ruffles was a less appropriate symbol of the years before 1914 than the chained prisoner, about to be executed, depicted on the poster by Henri de Toulouse-Lautrec. From one end of Europe to the other, executions were carried out in public squares by hanging or by guillotining, and everywhere they attracted spectators. The public taste for public punishment was great. Society was still close to a past in which physical violence had been considered exemplary. The gallows, after all, was only an extreme form of corporal punishment, and instilling fear was considered the best way of keeping order.

Indeed, the scaffold was set up in the public square with the consent of a whole generation. Barbarism was proclaimed and applauded during the *belle époque.*

In 1895 the Nobel Peace Prize was instituted. But who could believe in lasting peace? Nations, distrusting one another, had formed defensive military alliances. Austria, Germany, and Italy had joined in the Triple Alliance; France, Russia, and England had responded by forming the Triple Entente. On all continents, from the Nile to Afghanistan, from China to Cuba, there were areas of confrontation. The United States, long considered a peaceful nation intent on developing the land, went to war against Spain in 1898, installed itself in the Philippines, and took control of Cuba. In Africa European countries, especially France and England, continued their struggle for land and power—not always without resistance. Italy invaded Ethiopia in 1895 but was defeated in the Battle of Aduwa and withdrew. In the Boer War (1899–1902) the Boers (Dutch Africans) unsuccessfully tried to drive Great Britain from southern Africa. In China the nationalist Boxer Rebellion finally was crushed by an international force (Britain, France, Russia, Germany, Japan, and the United States) in 1900.

Countries were having their internal problems as well: there was anarchist violence in Spain, the Dreyfus affair in France, social troubles in Italy, and the revolution of 1905 in Russia, where there appeared resounding new names—such as Soviet, Trotsky, Bolshevik—whose long life no one then suspected.

In 1908 Bulgaria proclaimed its independence from Turkey; and nationalism made inroads in other regions. In 1911 Italy went to war with Turkey. France and Germany were in conflict about Morocco. Armies were stirring everywhere. The duration of compulsory military service was increased. War was imminent.

Of course these crises were only one aspect of the ferment that was to transform a whole way of life within those fifteen pre-war years. Many remarkable inventions that were to become part of everyday life had already appeared before the outbreak of World War I. These included the motion picture camera (the first movie theater was built in 1905); the airplane (the Wright brothers made their first flight in 1903); and the automobile (the first vehicle powered by an internal-combustion engine appeared in Germany in 1885).

Scientists were making revolutionary discoveries. In the cities middle-class houses were beginning to be lighted by electricity, which became the symbol of all the changes taking place and opened the way for many marvelous inventions. In 1898 Pierre and Marie Curie discovered radium. Albert Einstein formulated the theory of relativity in 1905. Guglielmo Marconi perfected the transmission of electromagnetic waves and as early as 1895 demonstrated the wireless telegraph.

In the face of scientific and technical progress and the confidence they engendered, those who warned of the threat of war and tried to check the race to armed conflict found only a small audience. A few powerful and eloquent voices, like that of

socialist Jean Léon Jaurès, futilely argued for world peace; Jaurès was killed by an assassin just before war engulfed Europe and then the world. Yet to those who came to know the hell of the trenches, the years between 1898 and 1914, violent and cruel as they were, could seem in retrospect only happy and peaceful—truly a *belle époque.*

This impression was not due entirely to nostalgia or to a comparison between war and peace. The years 1898 to 1914, despite the undercurrent of violence, were vigorous years of progress and expansion. Cities were the center of much of the excitement and activity. The city became a place for confrontation, a place where ideas were debated, where people first made contact with the new inventions of science and technology. Cities attracted people the world over: in 1850 there were 42 cities with more

than 100,000 inhabitants in Europe; in 1890 there were 118; in 1910, 183. In the United States the number of cities with more than 100,000 inhabitants grew from 32 in 1890 to 48 in 1910. On each continent there was at least one city with more than a million inhabitants. This phenomenon meant a final break with the rural way of life for hundreds of thousands of people.

It was primarily in the cities that major newspapers and books were published. Modern printing techniques—rotary presses and Linotype machines—facilitated the publication of large, inexpensive editions. Although the hand press remained in use in certain sectors of the printing industry, by the turn of the century newspapers and periodicals were being printed with the new machinery.

As newspapers became an increasingly important part of the street scene, posters

Right and below: poster by Edward Penfield for Harper's *magazine of February, 1895. Stuttgart, Staatsgalerie.*

advertising news stories covered public walls, and newsboys hawked the latest editions through the city streets of Europe and the United States. Strollers assembled around newspaper stands to read the boldly printed headlines. Thus faraway crises—the Russo-Japanese and Italo-Turkish wars, Anglo-French incidents, German intimidations—became known immediately. The public received the news head-on, and passions flared.

The habit of buying a daily paper grew among the urban population as the standard of living rose markedly. Although this higher standard of living did not immediately or uniformly affect the proletariat, the yoke of poverty gradually became lighter, and families could spend a part of their budget on such extras as newspapers and books.

The new reading habits took root all the more easily as illiteracy decreased. In France the law of 1882 that had made primary schooling compulsory, free, and secular was beginning to show results. By 1914 the number of illiterates had dropped to 2 per cent of the population, compared to 4 per cent in 1900 and 14 per cent in 1880. French children were kept in school until about the age of twelve. True, in other places, such as the south of Italy, similar efforts produced less satisfactory results. But in general people were beginning to read more.

The new urban way of life encouraged reading. One of the few ties among people was to share an event by reading about it in the newspaper. And reading helped pass the time on a subway or train trip. As the developing economy produced jobs that

Poster for G. P. Humphrey's secondhand bookstore in New York, about 1905. Printed by Peerless, New York. Paris, Musée des Arts Décoratifs.

Detail of a poster by Albert Sterner advertising a lending library for modern literature, 1903. Signed and dated at lower left. Stuttgart, Staatsgalerie.

Poster by Vaclav Oliva for the Prague paper Zlata Prahà, *about 1898. Printed by Unie, Prague, for the publisher Otty. Krefeld, Kaiser Wilhelm Museum.*

required less physical work and allowed more free time, reading became a familiar habit.

Since publishers wanted to appeal to the varied tastes of as many potential readers as possible, publications with licentious texts and illustrations began to appear in increasing numbers. This development showed how much the anonymity of city life favored the disintegration of puritanism, or of those moral principles that historically had been defended by both church and society.

In the cities bookshops advertised to attract customers. Because many readers were women, often women appeared on the advertisements. And since there had to be books to please female as well as male readers, love stories and stories of strange destinies were written to appeal to the middle-class urban woman, who because of the limited number of domestic duties she had to perform had both the time and the

Detail of a poster advertising The New York Times, *1895. At top right are the initials "EP" (perhaps for Edward Penfield). Paris, Musée des Arts Décoratifs.*

Poster by Ming for the poster printer Camis, 1910.
Paris, Musée des Arts Décoratifs.

need for the temporary escape that reading could provide.

But while it filled a gap in the lives of women living in a society still too traditional to allow them complete freedom, reading also was a step forward in women's liberation: the leisure to read newspapers and books gave women as well as men access to the outside world. At first this new access was available only to certain levels of society; at first it was only a vision of things to come.

In the area of social and political agitation the press played an increasingly important role. In France, for instance, conservative newspapers became especially influential as the public reacted to the anarchist movement. It was easy to exploit the fear of disorder in a big city such as Paris, which Émile Zola described in his novel of that name as a place where masses of

people acted only according to their passions. The activities of anarchists were always in evidence, and their unreasonable crimes served as pretexts for conservative attacks on the whole workers' movement.

While some anarchists were genuine criminals—leading a life of violence simply for the rewards of theft and murder—others saw in their own violent acts a means of achieving political and social ends. As one of them, Marius Jacob (who may have served as the model for Arsène Lupin, the hero of popular novels by Maurice Leblanc), said: "The fight will not be over until people share their joys and their troubles, their work and their wealth, until everything will belong to everyone." Despite the execution of such anarchists as François Ravachol in France in 1892 and Francisco Ferrer Guardia in Spain in 1909, the movement did not die. Financial scandals and exposure of the cor-

Poster by Aubrey Beardsley entitled The Pseudonym and Autonym Libraries, *for the publisher T. Fisher Unwin of London, 1895. There are many versions of this poster. Paris, Musée des Arts Décoratifs.*

AVBREY
BEARDSLEY

ruption of the parliamentary and political elite renewed public resentment. As one evidence that anarchism still had followers, in 1905 a magazine entitled *Anarchy* appeared in Paris.

Despite whatever idealistic causes the anarchist movement may have espoused and the high-minded motives of some of its members, it frightened people. The press in particular saw anarchism as sheer banditry. One poster advertising an antianarchist play showed a capped anarchist about to smash the skull of a woman after having killed her husband. Portraying the anarchist in a workingman's outfit forced the viewer to identify anarchism with the workers' movement: the cap became the symbol both of a class and of the dangers that class posed. In this poster, death, daggers, and a woman whom the anarchist worker seems about to rape reflect the fears of at least a part of society.

Such violent symbols were also used by the republican press, which grew as the workers' movement became better organized and as new trends appeared. One of these trends was anticlericalism. In a poster advertising *La Lanterne,* an anticlerical newspaper, a malevolent bird in clerical garb grips the church of Sacré-Coeur between his claws. To republicans Sacré-Coeur atop Montmartre symbolized the church's defiance of the republic and of the workers' movement, because its construction had been begun in 1875 partly as a public expiation for the crimes of the Commune.

This poster reveals the passion that animated both partisans and adversaries of clericalism. The very existence of an anticlerical press was proof enough that Catholicism no longer reigned alone. New ideologies—scientism, socialism, pragmatism—were replacing the teachings of the church.

Top: poster by Privat Livemont for the play Le Masque Anarchiste, by Montjuich, 1897. Signed and dated at right. Printed by Trommet et Staeves, Brussels. Paris, Musée des Arts Décoratifs.

Above: poster by Théophile Alexandre Steinlen advertising Le Journal's serialization of a novel by Émile Zola entitled Paris, 1897. Printed in Paris by Charles Verneau. Paris, Musée des Arts Décoratifs.

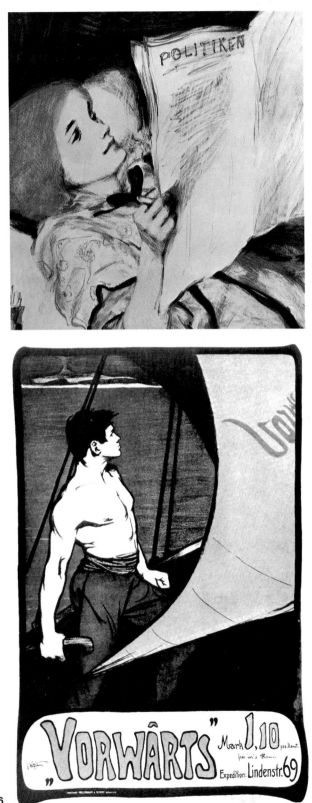

Catholicism did retain strongholds, particularly in the country and among the old aristocracy. It was to a certain extent responsible for the violent wave of anti-Semitism unleashed by the Dreyfus affair, for the army that convicted Jewish Captain Alfred Dreyfus of treason had always been conservative and Catholic. But the Dreyfus affair revealed not only the power of the old order but also the new power of the press. Without the press there would have been no Dreyfus affair. Without Zola's appeal in Clemenceau's paper *L'Aurore*, without his provocative "I accuse," there would have been no retrial and ultimate exoneration of Dreyfus. The battle over anti-Semitism was waged in the press and on posters. Partisan posters either called on Jews to boycott an anti-Semitic candidate or shrilly denounced Émile Zola. Newspaper headlines created the atmosphere of the streets, stimulated public opinion, and influenced political decisions.

Socialist newspapers began to appear at the end of the century. Posters invited the public to buy the Italian socialist paper *Avanti* or the German paper *Vorwärts*. In these posters the idealized middle-class woman who decorated so many posters was replaced by a virile man, stripped to the waist. Working-class viewers were inspired by the evocation of physical strength, the breaking chains, the sea, the sky, the rising sun. These symbols suggested an almost religious belief in the possibilities of a better, fairer, freer world.

Socialist newspapers grew with the rapid development of workers' organizations and the new importance of trade unions, which favored the spread of socialist ideas. From 1895 onward an economic revival created jobs for growing numbers of both blue-collar and white-collar workers. In France in 1866 there were 10 office workers for every 240 factory workers; in 1914 there were 10 for every 120. Between 1895 and 1914 wages increased, but since prices rose too, workers' purchasing power grew very slowly. Employers, however, profited con-

siderably in this period of economic boom.

In England in 1914, 85 per cent of the national wealth was in the hands of 5 per cent of the population. In France a million people owned 70 per cent of the national resources. While wages in the French mines increased 20 per cent, profits doubled. Moreover, as productivity increased, workers continued to be exploited. The greatest possible return on investment was the rule everywhere. Because a machine could execute a job in a fixed time, men were expected to adapt to similar schedules.

One can understand the feelings behind the railway workers' union poster that attacks the profits made by the railroad companies at the workers' expense. The owners of the company are represented as fat balloons wearing top hats, the trademark of the middle class. Workers were still approached on the basis of the old distinction between the fat and the thin, between those who had enough to eat and those who had not. One

can judge from these signs how divided society still was at the end of the nineteenth century. One can understand too why these workers, who had been called barbarians, went out on strike not only to demand better wages but to obtain a measure of recognition and dignity.

There were many strikes. In 1909 alone there were 1,537 in Germany, 1,205 in France, and 435 in England. In Italy in 1901 there were 1,400 strikes. Even agricultural workers began to be affected, and small landowners staged demonstrations. Governments everywhere were apprehensive of groups parading on May Day behind their red flags and singing the "International," which had been written by Eugène Pottier during the Bloody Week of the Commune. On Bloody Sunday in Russia, January 22, 1905, strikers were cut down by Cossacks, setting in motion the first revolution in the land of the czars.

Unions and labor exchanges were formed

Anonymous propaganda poster of the French railway workers' union, about 1910. The words in the center read: "Is it just that those who risk nothing should have everything and those who risk their lives every day should have nothing?" Private collection.

Poster by Frank B. Master for the May issue of the monthly Scribner's, *about 1900. Paris, Musée des Arts Décoratifs.*

Anonymous poster from the early 1900's for the Compagnie Générale Transatlantique advertising weekly departures from Le Havre to New York, departures to the West Indies and South America, and Mediterranean cruises. Printed in Paris by Dupuis. Paris, Musée des Arts Décoratifs.

in various countries. There were four million union members in England and two and a half million in Germany. In France and Italy the unions were strongly socialist and anarchist. Despite profound differences between the anarchists and the socialists, despite controversies about the direction union action should take, and despite the differences between unions in England and on the Continent, labor was truly becoming organized. Modern industry, which had created great concentrations of workers, facilitated labor organization, and emigration helped make unionism an international phenomenon. During the last years of the century, tens of millions of people, particularly from the Mediterranean countries and central Europe, moved to the United States. Many others left France and the British Isles for those countries' colonies.

Transportation continued to undergo transformation. Railroads became very important in these years. Rail tunnels were blasted through the Alps: the Mont Cenis was opened in 1871, the Saint Gotthard in 1882, and in 1906 the Simplon, which made possible the Paris–Milan rail link and opened the Italian lakes to tourism. The world network of tracks grew from 187,500 miles in 1875 to 687,500 in 1913. In the United States and Canada railroads joined the coasts. Chile and Argentina were linked by rail. Siberia was spanned, and men dreamed of a railway across the Sahara. The line from "the Cape to Cairo" had already been begun, its steel girders thrown across the gorges. The railroad was a subject for poetry: the locomotive became a powerful, rampaging beast burrowing through the mountains, with man its rider and master. The imagery suggests man's dream of conquering the earth with machines and his fascination with building.

The impact of the railroad was far-reaching. Lower ticket prices and freight charges (they decreased by 50 per cent in half a century) soon made the railroad the key means of transport. The expansion of the railroad encouraged agricultural special-

French poster advertising electric trams. Signed "G. Koisted" at lower left. Paris, Musée des Arts Décoratifs.

Detail from a poster entitled Wanda by Aleardo Terzi
for a seaside resort near Savona, Italy, about 1900.
Printed by Arti Grafiche, Bergamo. Treviso, Museo
Civico Luigi Bailo, Salce Collection.

ization: certain types of grains came to be grown only in regions where their yield was greatest, with the harvest then distributed by train. Railroads became an instrument of Western penetration into underdeveloped areas, thus prompting political rivalries. The granting to the Germans of the concession for the Baghdad Railway in 1899, for instance, was considered a defeat for the English.

By the turn of the century ships had been so improved that their schedules were largely independent of adverse weather. Posters advertised "departures every Saturday from Le Havre directly to New York." Both passenger and cargo ships boasted iron hulls, propellers, and above all steam boilers. As early as 1914, 90 per cent of the world's warships were powered by coal-fed steam boilers. Ships became larger and larger: the German passenger ship *Vaterland*, launched in 1914, weighed 60,000 tons. The Suez Canal opened in 1869, the Corinth Canal in 1893, the Kiel Canal in 1895, and the Panama Canal in 1914. The links between countries and continents were proliferating.

The era of travel had begun. Trains ran on schedule through quiet countrysides, and large passenger ships departed regularly from quays. People were becoming more mobile because travel was both comfortable and relatively free of risks. Trains had sleeping and dining cars; passenger ships were floating hotels. Some travelers were rich: globetrotting millionaires and veiled adventuresses, often expatriates, traveled on international trains and steamers. Others who could not travel quite so elegantly also became expatriates, perhaps looking for an easier life or the chance to make a fortune elsewhere. The poorest travelers, the steerage passengers to America, were not particularly moved by the romance of travel. Yet their hopes too were attached to the curls of smoke issuing from the stacks of locomotives and steamers.

Immigrants poured into America. Europeans remained the favored immigrants, and Anglo-Saxon and Germanic groups were preferred over Mediterranean peoples. Those from Asia were less welcome, and legal barriers in the form of limited quotas were raised against incoming Japanese and Chinese. During the first years of the twentieth century the majority of immigrants seeking the mythical riches of the American continent came from the Iberian and Italian peninsulas. They were joined by Jews fleeing pogroms and Slavs fleeing hunger and political persecution.

Between 1901 and 1913 Brazil and Argentina received three million immigrants, most of them Italian and Spanish. During the same twelve years the United States took in twenty million, of whom more than 50 per cent were Italians, Slavs, and Jews.

There were smaller migrations within Europe, facilitated by the opening of new railway lines. People moved from the country into the cities; seven million Russians installed themselves in Siberia, the Caucasus, and central Asia; Italians moved to France, where population growth had slowed.

That the poor should prefer exile to misery at home was a new attitude, particularly on such a large scale. Not just the most adven-

שפייז וועט געווינען די קריעג!

אדער קומט אהער צו געפינען פרייהייט.

יעצט מוזט אדער העלפען זיא צו בעשיצען.

מיר מוזען די עלליים פערזארגען מיט וייץ.

לאזט קיין זאך ניט גיין אין נוועץ

יונייטעד סטייטס שפייז פערוואלטונג.

An anonymous poster for a German bicycle called the Meteor, about 1910. Stuttgart, Staatsgalerie.

Below: detail of a W. H. Bradley poster for Victor bicycles, about 1900. Printed by Fortes, Boston. Paris, Musée des Arts Décoratifs.

turous members of a community left; entire communities migrated with their women, old people, and children. Families, neighborhoods, and social structures were soon affected; poor areas became deserted, and the exodus from the country brought about the death of ancient villages.

For the well-to-do traveling might simply mean leaving the city in the summer for the country or the seashore. The pleasure of gathering in Venice, on the Mediterranean coast between Cannes and San Remo, or on the Channel coast at Deauville was reserved for a small elite. Once on the beach, one sought the comfort of a large wicker beach chair. Bathing suits were chaste, and even children were covered up when they played in the sand. Women took part in this leisure world. They were shown on posters with their faces in perfect order, their hair carefully combed despite the ocean waves. Sport did not interfere with their appearance.

Women also rode bicycles, which were a great success after they were perfected in the 1880's. The development of the chain drive in 1885 and the pneumatic tire in 1889 made possible the marketing of a simple, efficient, inexpensive machine. With the first Tour de France, organized in 1903, bicycling became a true sport.

As the bicycle business boomed, posters advertising the new machines proliferated. Some showed women touring with men. One romantic vision showed a nymphlike creature flying away with a winged bike. And an ad for Peugeot bicycles showed two soldiers, one on horseback, the other with a bike—suggesting that the bike was as noble a steed as the horse.

The appearance of women in bicycle posters indicates their importance to manufacturers as potential buyers. In fact, the bicycle proved an early step in the liberation of women by making them more mobile and independent. The women who took up the bicycle when it was still a relative novelty were obviously middle class; but since they also guided taste and set the tone, the turn

Left and below: poster by E. Vulliemin for Peugeot bicycles, about 1900. Signed at lower right. Paris, Musée des Arts Décoratifs.

Right: poster advertising the New York Ledger, *about 1900. Paris, Musée des Arts Décoratifs.*

Below: poster by Massias for Gladiator bicycles, about 1905. Paris, Musée des Arts Décoratifs.

of the century became a starting point in the emancipation of all women.

Horses were still widely used; armies, for instance, had companies of scouts on bicycles, but they had whole battalions of cavalry. Gradually, however, the horse was becoming a showpiece. In the past horses had been so commonplace that they had drawn no particular attention in the streets. Now, however, they became symbols of luxury. Horseback and carriage riding became social attributes; the bicycle was middle class. Posters show ladies in top hats taking lessons in horsemanship as others would take lessons in etiquette.

As if to emphasize the differences between the days of the horse-drawn carriage and those of trams, buses, bicycles, and private automobiles, hippodromes became the settings for historical pageants featuring warriors on horseback. As society evolved toward the machine, horses appeared increasingly in public spectacles.

Sports and outdoor activities grew in popularity during this period. If urban life was beginning to separate man from nature and if the machine was replacing the horse, men never stopped seeking to re-establish their contact with the sea and to conquer mountains. In France the Alpine Club was

Two anonymous French posters advertising trotting races and a riding school. Not dated. Paris, Musée des Arts Décoratifs.

Poster by Edward Penfield for the New York City store Heller and Bachrach, about 1900. Signed at lower left. Paris, Musée des Arts Décoratifs.

OVERLEAF: poster by O. Orazi advertising an equestrian entertainment at the Hippodrome on the Boulevard de Clichy in Paris, about 1905. Signed at lower right. Paris, Musée des Arts Décoratifs.

English poster of 1906 announcing a public discussion of the Russian revolution of 1905 at Memorial Hall. Private collection.

founded in 1874 and the Touring Club in 1890. Even the Baedeker guidebooks—those fabulous travelers' handbooks to most of Europe and much of the rest of the world—contained mountain-climbing itineraries. Travelers were looking not only for nature but for physical exercise—skiing and skating, for example. The interest in sailing, rowing, and tennis, which originated in Anglo-Saxon countries, soon conquered the Continent. As one consequence of sports and tourism, whole regions were changed and new industries were started.

Because one had to have leisure time to indulge in them, these new recreations were initially the prerogative of the well-to-do, a minority who pursued them enthusiastically and snobbishly. Eventually, however, the middle class began to rediscover its lost taste for physical exercise. And since the middle class was the model, growing num-

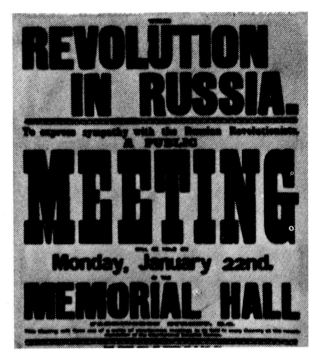

REVOLUTION IN RUSSIA.

To express sympathy with the Russian Revolutionists

A PUBLIC

MEETING

Monday, January 22nd.

MEMORIAL HALL

Poster by Ernst Neumann advertising Sosa tennis balls, made by Sorge und Sabeck of Berlin, 1908. Printed by Hollerbaum und Schmidt, Berlin. Krefeld, Kaiser Wilhelm Museum.

bers of people, particularly young people, found their way to the beaches and the stadiums, as well as to the rougher outdoors. In 1894 Pierre de Coubertin revived the Olympic games. In 1908 the Boy Scouts was founded. Sports and the outdoor life had become popular as well as fashionable.

In the cities the standards of public morality were changing. People, and especially women, began enjoying greater freedom. The rich, the talented, and those who lived on the fringes of society shared a common goal: to enjoy life. Passions were no longer held in check by considerations of morals or background. The demimondaine, the prostitute, and the adventuress became social and literary types. One met them in salons and in cafés. The "easy girl" with vague eyes and naked shoulders, passive and inviting, soon became a subject for posters.

The café became a popular gathering spot. It was a place where people could meet and lose their anonymity—a refuge, as has often been said, for lonely souls. With its polished copper bar, its mirrors, its music, and its liveliness, the café welcomed the passer-by. And with the help of alcohol, the warmth of the setting penetrated heart and soul. For some, alcohol induced a temporary and artificial cheerfulness that was the only kind they could afford.

Women came to the cafés—not only

Opposite: detail of a poster by V. Ceccanti for one of the first Italian espresso machines, about 1900. Treviso, Museo Civico Luigi Bailo, Salce Collection.

Two posters from the Museo Civico Luigi Bailo, Treviso: Marcello Dudovich, Fratelli Sanguinetti, *c.1900; Leopoldo Metlicovitz,* Mele, *c.1910.*

those whose profession it was to wait for a customer's attentions, but middle-class women who no longer hesitated to enter after a day of shopping. As an indication of the growing freedom that women enjoyed and the changing concepts of propriety and of public morality, women on posters invited consumers to buy absinthe, beer, coffee, or champagne.

Paris, which had recovered from the devastating effects of the Franco-Prussian War, became the center of European frivolity. It was not just a thriving, bustling city; it was a city of high spirits, where the rich and the demimonde mingled happily and effortlessly in search of entertainment and fun. The center of Paris night life was Montmartre. There such thriving cafés as the famous Moulin Rouge presented popular concerts that were a combination of music-hall and nightclub entertainments. All the best

Detail of a poster by Hans Rudi Erdt for Kloss & Foerster champagne, 1912. Signed at top left. Printed in Berlin by Hollerbaum und Schmidt. Stuttgart, Staatsgalerie.

people in Paris went to music halls such as the Folies-Bergère. Artists too were a prominent part of the Montmartre scene. One of them, Henri de Toulouse-Lautrec, captured on posters the spirit of the gay, frenzied, often debauched life in which he so actively participated.

The cancan, featuring ruffles and lace and dancers kicking their legs in the air or bending low over customers, came to symbolize the tastes of a whole generation. (Of course certain segments of society, such as the conservative middle class and the aristocracy, were indignant about these "daring" spectacles.) Male dancers were rare. Only girls were on stage, all alike, wearing the same feathers, doing the same steps in unison. It was impossible to single one out. Their anonymity was deliberate: to the rich nightclub patron, women were interchangeable, dressed up for him, dancing for him. Legs were more important than faces, as

the poster advertising the Scala in Paris makes clear.

There were also other forms of entertainment. The opera and the operetta remained popular, and music and theater underwent a renaissance. In music French composers Claude Debussy (1862–1918) and Maurice Ravel (1875–1937) led a movement that was a reaction to the drama and emotionalism of Richard Wagner's romantic music. Their new school, known as impressionism and inspired by the French impressionist painters, concentrated on creating atmosphere and mood. Another influential innovator, Hungarian composer Béla Bartók (1881–1945), stressed the use of folk themes in his music, which combined atonality with traditional methods of composition.

Music was no longer confined to concert halls. The middle class became fond of what they believed to be an aristocratic habit: playing the piano. At the beginning of the

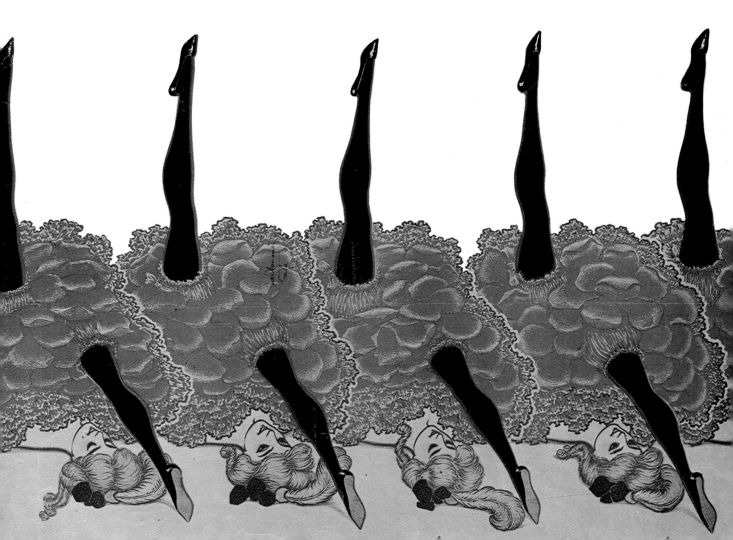

Right: two anonymous posters for entertainments at the Folies-Bergère: one featuring the boxer James J. Corbett, and the other the variety-show performer Cléo de Mérode. Paris, Musée des Arts Décoratifs.

Below: detail from a poster by Roedel for the Moulin Rouge, 1897. Signed at lower right. Printed by Chaix, Paris. This poster exists in different colors and with different texts. Paris, Musée des Arts Décoratifs.

century the piano had captivated only the upper middle class, but as the years passed its popularity spread. Every middle-class sitting room contained a piano at which the daughter or the lady of the house played songs before applauding guests. The imitation and diffusion of customs and cultural habits through the various levels of society had become the rule.

The democratization of the theater was signaled by the success of light plays inspired by opera or operetta. The taste of many at the turn of the century favored clever, fluffy entertainment with a bawdy undertone or plays about romantic heroes. Edmond Rostand was a particularly popular playwright, and his plays—especially *Cyrano de Bergerac* (1898) and *L'Aiglon* (1900), a play about Napoleon's son—were enthusiastically received. These elicited applause not just from the upper middle

Anonymous poster for a show at the Chicago Opera House, about 1900. Paris, Musée des Arts Décoratifs.

Poster by Dudley Hardy for The Yeomen of the Guard *at the Savoy Theater in London, about 1893. Signed at lower right. Paris, Musée des Arts Décoratifs.*

class but also from the lower middle class, whose members adored family melodramas, often about adulteries that they would not dare to commit. These audiences loved modern morality plays and the histrionics of the actors.

But all over Europe the theater was undergoing a revolution at the beginning of the century. Much of what was being presented on the stage was innovative and experimental. In 1887 André Antoine founded the Théâtre Libre, where works of the naturalist school were presented and new dramatic techniques tried; Antoine's theater became a model for experimental theaters in Europe and the United States. Jacques Copeau, another leader, in 1913 established the Théâtre du Vieux Colombier. Copeau, who also was interested in new stage techniques, produced poetic dramas and was the first to use symbolic set designs. He too was influential in the modern theater. In 1909 the Russian ballet impresario Sergei

Below: a poster by V. Bignami for Giacomo Puccini's opera Manon Lescaut, about 1895. Signed at lower left. Printed by Ricordi, Milan. Private collection.

Diaghilev went to Paris with a troupe of Russian dancers and founded the Ballet Russe, which revolutionized the world of dance. Pablo Picasso, Marc Chagall, and André Derain designed sets for the Ballet Russe; Claude Debussy, Maurice Ravel, and Igor Stravinsky were among those who wrote music for the company.

As always, certain actors and actresses were idolized by the public. While idolatry was hardly a novelty, the press and photography spread the reputation of stars farther than had ever been possible by such traditional means as posters. One of the biggest stars was Sarah Bernhardt (1844–1923), who dominated the French stage and toured the rest of Europe and the United States. One of her popular triumphs was

L'Aiglon, written for her by Edmond Rostand. One typical poster advertised "the divine Sarah's" appearance in Medea at the Théâtre de la Renaissance. Such posters helped make the names and faces of stars familiar.

As the twentieth century progressed, social and political tensions increased. Unemployment and taxation became increasingly explosive issues, frequently leading to strikes and demonstrations. Strikes often became confrontations with the army: drums rolled and bugles sounded as soldiers charged and fired. In Milan, for instance, from May 6 to May 9, 1898, unemployed workers battled the police and the army. During the outbreak more than a hundred were killed. In retaliation an anar-

MANON LESCAUT

DRAMMA LIRICO DI G. PUCCINI

MILANO-OFFICINE G. RICORDI &C.
Proprietà riservata

V. Bignami

chist assassinated King Umberto of Italy in 1900.

Competition between the industrial countries intensified. One of the nations most threatened by competition was England: the United States and especially Germany were chipping away at its industrial and commercial supremacy. England was paying dearly for having been the first country to experience the industrial revolution. Its machinery had become obsolete; emigration deprived it of many of its most dynamic and inventive men. About 1900 the country was overrun by tenacious, efficient traveling salesmen from Germany who offered quality goods at competitive prices. In 1897 a German passenger liner beat the records that England's Cunard Line ships had held for the transatlantic crossing.

Reaction in England was strong. Posters reflected a growing resentment toward foreigners and imports. One poster showed shops full of goods imported from all over the Continent; a poster man carries a sand-wich board announcing a pro–free-trade meeting where only foreigners will be speakers, while in the background the unemployed demonstrate.

This political poster was in support of the protectionist tariff legislation proposed by Liberal-Unionist-Conservative leader Joseph Chamberlain, who tried to reverse the traditional British policy of free trade by imposing tariffs in an effort to restore British commercial supremacy. But the Labour party opposed protectionist policies because they entailed higher prices and broader taxation, the burden of which would fall on the working class. Both sides pleaded their case in posters. In the 1906 elections Chamberlain's Conservatives were badly defeated.

In the battle over tariffs posters were a political weapon. Some were quite realistic, others more symbolic, like the one in which Chamberlain rolls the barrel of "taxation" over a worker. Posters appealed to reason as well as to the imagination, and in a sense they summarized political arguments. In that sense they could be dan-

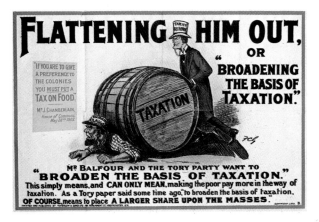

gerous, because their direct, exaggerated arguments became fixed in the public mind. Posters were replaced, but their slogans lingered. The use of posters for propaganda was being refined.

The striking thing in these propaganda posters—quite apart from the English controversy over tariffs—was the growing hatred of foreigners and foreign goods. This development was not peculiar to England: xenophobic and racist propaganda was yet another expression of the nationalism growing in all European countries. One aspect of this hatred, anti-Semitism, in 1896 led the Austrian Theodor Herzl to publish *The Jewish State; an Attempt at a Modern Solution of the Jewish Problem*, which advocated the creation of a Jewish homeland in Palestine and was the origin of the Zionist movement.

In England nationalism flowered as a result of commercial rivalry with the German empire of Kaiser Wilhelm II. Elsewhere it took root among oppressed minorities who wanted the establishment of their own states, or found expression in a romantic glorification of fatherland, race, and national traditions. The press, serialized novels, and posters contributed to the spread of these nationalist feelings. The masses were stirred by military processions and by articles and slogans holding "the other side" responsible for unemployment, poverty, or injustice.

FAUST

OPERA IN 5. ATTI

MUSICA DI

C. GOUNOD

The urban masses, particularly middle-class women, continued their spirited consumption of new products. It was difficult to imagine a cataclysm occurring when life was full of promise and the streets were full of posters advertising so many luxuries and conveniences for sale. The benefits bestowed by the industrial revolution filled people with confidence. Despite rumblings by the workers' parties, despite the first Russian revolution, the middle class was still firmly in control, and the well-to-do had an easy life.

It made sense to own stocks, for currencies were stable and interest was paid regularly on money invested. It was marvelous to be able to buy automobiles and cameras and to enjoy all the new products that made life more comfortable. Advertising began to concern itself with the most intimate areas; nothing was concealed when sales were at stake. One American

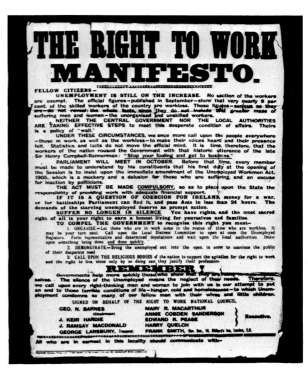

Right: poster by A. Mazza advertising the photography shop of M. Ganzini, 1912. Treviso, Museo Civico Luigi Bailo, Salce Collection.

poster advertised toilet paper. Another advertising a January sale of lingerie and linen at a Chicago store showed a comfortable middle-class bedroom, not luxurious but well appointed.

Goods had to be sold, and therefore new motivations and occasions for buying were created. The January white sale was invented to stimulate business after Christmas. The white sale kept the shops going until after Easter, when people had an excuse to go shopping again of their own accord.

There were no shortages in economically advanced countries or among the well-to-do. The new problem was how to dispose of surplus merchandise. Businesses had to find new customers and take advantage of every selling technique that might lead people to buy. Before a washing machine

Above: detail of a poster by B. Martin Justice for Quad cameras, about 1900. Signed. Paris, Musée des Arts Décoratifs.

Below: detail of a poster by Henry Muenier for Star-light soap, 1899. Printed by De Rycher, Brussels. Paris, Musée des Arts Décoratifs.

could be successfully marketed, the housewife had to be sold on wringing out laundry by machine, instead of with the hands that had sufficed previously.

One of the important untapped sources of new customers was the children's market. The children shown on posters were no longer simply smaller versions of their elders; they were depicted as having their own needs and requiring their own special products, such as food and soap. These posters reflect a new relationship between children and parents. By addressing advertisements directly to children, focusing on them as potential "customers," advertising helped modify the long-standing authoritarian structure of the family.

Families shrank in size. To have only one child was no longer exceptional, particularly in middle-class families; and the trend was toward two or three children. Formerly the concept of the family had extended to uncles, aunts, and cousins, particularly in the country, but this was no longer true in the cities. Where before he had been just one among many, the child became the center of family life. The middle-class child, often raised in an apartment with limited space, was his mother's pride and hope for the future.

This new attitude toward children had become possible at least in part because environment and living conditions had changed. Parents no longer needed many children to work on the farm. Also, the infant's life was less frequently in danger during his first days. And as infant mortality decreased, parents no longer needed to have many children in order to insure that at least some survived.

Infant mortality had declined because of recent medical discoveries and a higher standard of living. Important new medical and surgical procedures, developed during the last years of the nineteenth century, led to the control or even the disappearance of certain diseases. The discovery of antiseptics and vitamins helped doctors master diseases that had always claimed children first.

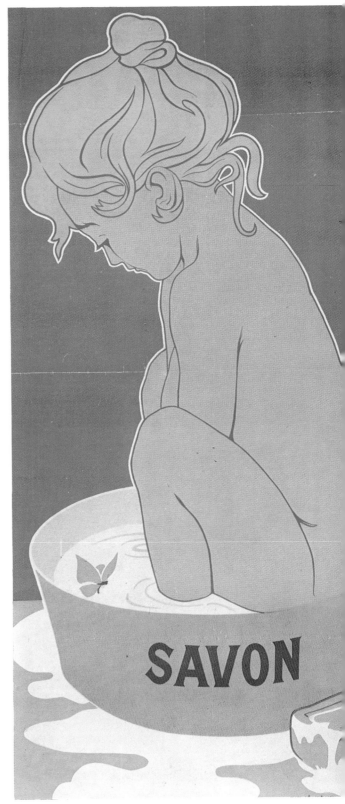

Below: anonymous poster for the Morgan Envelope Company, about 1900. Printed in Paris by Chaix. Paris, Musée des Arts Décoratifs.

Bottom: detail of a poster by Bru for the Christmas number of the San Francisco monthly Sunset, *1903. Paris, Musée des Arts Décoratifs.*

Opposite: detail of a poster for a January linen sale at the Chicago store Carson Pirie Scott, about 1903. Paris, Musée des Arts Décoratifs.

Fat, healthy children figured on posters as the symbols of joy and hope. In fact, parents projected their unfulfilled desires onto their children, an indication that the general attitude toward life had changed. Life expectancy had increased. Epidemics and famines had almost completely disappeared, at least in Europe. Society became more mobile, and at least for city dwellers everything changed in the space of a few years. Shortages had been replaced not only by abundance but also by variety. Streets that had always been dark were ablaze with light. People felt reassured and began to believe that many things were possible.

Advertisers were quick to note this change, reinforcing it and using it to their advantage. They understood that the key word for the early twentieth century, the word that would entice people to buy, was "modern." But because mobility and change had become characteristic of the times, the definition of "modern" kept changing. To stay modern was an effort that required constant work.

One fashionable "modern" style of about 1900 was art nouveau, a highly ornamental style characterized by arabesques and interlacing spirals. In the 1890's it began to appear in a wide variety of products. In furniture and in architecture cast iron and steel became more widely used. The entrances to the Métro (subway) in Paris were decorated with fashionable art nouveau metal foliage. Posters as well as ceramics were decorated with stylized floral motifs. Jewelry and knickknacks also had the interlacing curves and sinuous lines of the new style. Women wore floral jewelry and had their hair elaborately coiled. They too became "modern" objects, fashionable knickknacks among other fashionable knickknacks.

The constant changes in fashion, dictated with a view to higher sales, made greater demands on women. All parts of their outer wardrobe had to be fashionable. Shoes, for instance, which had been hidden

under long skirts for so many years, came out into the open; instead of being simply utilitarian, they were an important part of a fashionable wardrobe. And changes in fashion encouraged women to buy new shoes before they had worn out their old ones. Of course this pleased shoe manufacturers, who experimented with new materials from which to make shoes.

Women felt a similar desire to own up-to-the-minute dresses, corsets, and large hats, which threw the face into shadow and enhanced its mystery. As far as women's clothes were concerned nothing was merely utilitarian any longer: everything became ornament, even a corset that no one except the wearer was likely ever to see. Looking in her bedroom mirror, a woman was forced to compare herself with the models she saw every day on posters. And the man with her was naturally tempted to make the same comparison, which acted as an additional incentive for the woman to conform to current fashions in order to come as close as possible to the "ideal" of the model. In short, the developing influence of fashion imposed new restrictions. On the other hand, the body was liberated as clothes became simpler and more closely fitted to a woman's natural shape.

Men were not subject to the rapid changes in fashion that confronted women. Their clothes did not change quite so much in style, and the evolutions were in the direction of simplicity. Until 1880 the only competition to the frock coat had been the jacket. But by 1900 the frock coat had disappeared. The cumbersome top hat, for a long time the symbol of the middle class, was forced out by the bowler hat, the boater, and sometimes the cap, when it was an elegant one worn for traveling.

Men's hair fashions changed as well. Beards were becoming a distant memory. Razors were no longer expensive, thanks to the evolution of metallurgy, the invention of various types of steel, and mass production of blades. The chemical industry produced the soap whose wide distribution made daily shaving possible. Posters, ad-

vertisements, and photographs made the clean-shaven face familiar, and from the end of the century onward young men in particular adopted the beardless look. Many men wore mustaches, but their hair was cut short, and the long vogue for bushy sideburns was gradually dying out. As always, social pressure to conform to current styles was strong.

A whole web of causes was responsible for these changes in fashion—from tech-

nological developments to changes in living habits. For instance, those who lived in cities traveled frequently by public transport and required simpler clothes so that they could move nimbly and fit comfortably into relatively crowded places.

Furthermore, the appearance of large groups of salaried people such as sales and service personnel made a certain uniformity necessary. Their clothes were mass produced and therefore had to be simpler in order to fit the greatest number of people reasonably well without extensive alterations. The two- or three-piece ready-made suit became the working outfit for the lower-middle-class man. It was always gray or black and without embellishments, and as such it suited the personalities of people who could not or would not express themselves—people caught up in the routine of their monotonous jobs.

Thus men tended to fade into anonymity **89**

ing and hunting, or spent their time at the races and in the paddock or at the beach could elect not to wear the gray or black uniforms of the crowds milling about the city streets. These modish rich often followed the fashion as assiduously as women. They decreed what was elegant in men's clothes. But while most middle-class women— encouraged by advertising and mass production—tried to be fashionable, most men remained indifferent to the constant changes of style decreed by the few playboys who had the leisure to care.

One reason for the difference was that most men worked, and society expected them to concentrate on their professions. Fantasy was considered the prerogative of women, artists, and bohemians, not of middle-class men. Furthermore, the lower-middle-class man was often an employee or a civil servant (in France the number of civil servants increased by 70 per cent between 1870 and 1900); and in such professions originality in clothes was discouraged.

at the same time that women—first of all middle-class women, then gradually others —were decking themselves out seductively in the latest fashions, which increasingly flattered and accentuated their figures. Men's bodies seemed to be unimportant, hidden as they were by their suits, those functional social uniforms. It was not a man's appearance but his place in society or business that counted. His clothing indicated this status.

There were exceptions to the general uniformity of dress, of course. The men who frequented Monte Carlo, went pigeon shoot-

Consequently men had to express their individuality in attitudes and habits that women did not dare adopt. Here, too, advertising encouraged people to take up certain new habits. Smoking was one of them.

Detail of a poster by Ernst Deutsch for the German shoe firm Salamander, 1912. Signed and dated at lower left. Stuttgart, Staatsgalerie.

Four posters from the Museo Civico Luigi Bailo in Treviso. Left to right: Aleardo Villa for Müller sewing machines, about 1900; anonymous poster for the Naples clothing store Mele, 1911; two posters by Marcello Dudovich, also for Mele, 1914. Details appear at bottom and opposite.

Of course people had used tobacco long before the beginning of the twentieth century. It was taken as snuff, chewed, and smoked in pipes. The novelty of this century was cigarettes, both factory made and those rolled by the smoker. With the twentieth century cigarette smoking became an attribute of the modern man, an apparently harmless pursuit that was nevertheless habit-forming.

Once the middle class had taken up smoking the habit spread quickly. Workers, beginning with the young ones, smoked cigarettes to show that they had broken out of their class. Already they were copying the middle class by shaving each morning, by abandoning the cap for the boater on Sundays, and by wearing a jacket instead of a smock to work. Smoking cigarettes also helped them believe that they were rising above their class.

In fact the availability of cheap mass-produced clothes and the abandonment of the top hat and frock coat were eroding visible class distinctions between urban men. The working-class aristocracy, for example, mixed with the lower middle class and adopted its habits and appearance. Naturally this apparent leveling was taking place only in countries where at least some of the profits realized through mass production were reaching all classes, including workers, thus making accessible to them important material advantages. This was not the case in Russia and central Europe,

Posters by Leopoldo Metlicovitz (left) and Marcello Dudovich (right) for Mele, 1913–14. Treviso, Museo Civico Luigi Bailo.

or in Europe's African and Asian colonies.

Now that some distinctions between classes were becoming blurred, the integration of workers into the mainstream of society could really begin. But again this did not take place in all countries, or among the whole of the working class in any given country. It was rather that the workers who were best off gradually slipped into the middle class, whose habits and clothes they had already adopted. In recognition of this development, Lenin spoke about the establishment of "middle-class workers' parties." In his novel *Germinal,* Émile Zola described a militant union member who climbed socially, acquired new responsibilities, and became a member of Parliament.

This form of integration was particularly marked in countries with a strong democratic tradition, such as England, or countries where industrial development was particularly vigorous, such as Germany. It became possible because the most ambitious of the workers were convinced that with a bit of luck they could climb the social ladder, that the lower rungs were still open, and that compulsory free education would allow their sons to acquire at least the elements of culture. Thus they gradually moved into the lower middle class. In the Western countries a classic situation developed in which the peasant left his land, installed himself in a provincial town, attained a certain standard of living by working for a salary, and then sent his son to the big city or had him become a teacher. This situation

Poster by Lucian Bernhard for the Russian firm Provodnik, 1913. The poster was made in Berlin. Stuttgart, Staatsgalerie.

Poster by Ludwig Hohlwein for Kehl, a Neuchâtel clothing store. Printed by J. E. Wolfensberger, Zurich. Darmstadt, Hessisches Landesmuseum.

Poster by Hans Rudi Erdt for Problem cigarettes, 1912. Signed and dated at lower left. Printed by Hollerbaum und Schmidt, Berlin. Krefeld, Kaiser Wilhelm Museum.

Poster for a German firm of hatmakers, about 1915. Stuttgart, Staatsgalerie.

was particularly typical in France, where on the eve of World War I it was instrumental in strengthening national unity.

The city was the center of these developments. At the beginning of the twentieth century there was a greater difference between a peasant and a city dweller than between two city dwellers.

City dwellers of all classes could not help being aware of the changes that were taking place in customs, ideas, fashions, and styles. A poster, a building, or a sculpture could open new horizons. As the rectilinear drawing in the poster for Laferme cigarettes of Dresden indicates, even by the end of the century the time of arabesques and harmonious volutes was passing and the age of geometric design was beginning. In architecture in particular, architects in Germany, England, France, and the United States experimented with austere new geometric forms. The use of reinforced concrete made it possible to erect tall buildings with clean lines; by 1908 there were already several skyscrapers in the United States, the highest of which had forty-five stories. In the nineteenth century art and engineering had had opposing aims; in the twentieth they were unified.

The chief proponent of the new "functional" architecture was German architect Walter Gropius. Gropius' model factory at the Cologne Exposition of 1914, using as it did large expanses of glass and utilizing modern engineering techniques, exemplified the vigor of this new school, which wanted to bring art and industry together. In Weimar in 1919 Gropius founded the Bauhaus, a revolutionary art school that combined the study of pure arts with that of science and technology and stressed functional applications and the problems of mass production. Among the Bauhaus faculty were Paul Klee, Lyonel Feininger, Vasili Kandinski, László Moholy-Nagy, and Marcel Breuer. With their emphasis on the cooperation among art, science, and technology, the Bauhaus ideas revolutionized design.

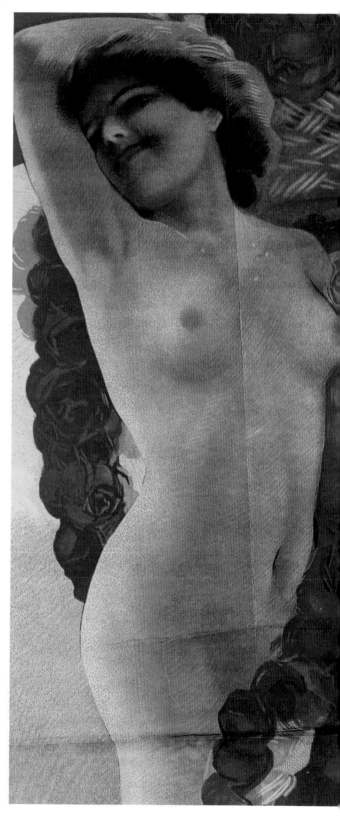

The change taking place in architecture had in turn been influenced by an evolution away from realism in the visual arts. In painting the new geometric ideas found expression in the sensational movement called cubism, which in turn had been influenced by the works of late-nineteenth-century postimpressionists, especially Paul Cézanne. Cézanne believed that "nature must be treated in terms of the cylinder, the sphere, the cone." Carrying out his idea, the cubists, led by Pablo Picasso, overturned traditional ideas of space and plane in an effort to explore the underlying structure of reality.

The rigid geometry of concrete buildings and of cubist paintings was the antithesis of impressionism, of the imprecise. Even people who might not have frequented painting exhibitions became aware of the new way of depicting and seeing the world, because its influence was visible in the streets.

One sign was the appearance of naked figures on posters. The bodies were often still draped, but the lines were sharp. In women the breasts were clearly depicted. Some of these figures appeared as they traditionally had, in romantic or heroic settings or along with mythological references. In

Detail from a poster by Leopoldo Metlicovitz for an internal-combustion engine, 1905. Treviso, Museo Civico Luigi Bailo, Salce Collection.

Detail from a poster by Adolfo de Carolis entitled Ramon Escudo, 1912. Treviso, Museo Civico Luigi Bailo, Salce Collection.

MEISENBACH, RIFFARTH & Cs MÜNCHEN.

ST VND DEKORATION

one striking design—an almost surrealist advertisement for an Italian brand of ink—the realism of the figure is combined with less realistic decorative elements. Another, an advertisement for a German art magazine, featured the hard lines, the sharp contrasts, and the lighting used by postimpressionists.

There had of course always been statues and paintings depicting naked men, but these were usually heroic scenes or stories from mythology. Now naked bodies were being used to call attention to a product. It was yet another sign of how customs were changing.

Western Europe as a whole was becoming anxious, and it was developing a taste for the morbid. The forces disputing rationalism were growing, casting doubt on the value of scientific knowledge, delighting in anxiety, and evoking death. When the suggestive cover of a periodical entitled *Science for Everyone* showed the effects of x-rays, its intention was not so much to illustrate a scientific process as to elicit the enduring fear of death. The impact of such pessimism was all the stronger because it reached an ever wider public as a result of mass distribution.

A sense of disquiet that had for a while been stilled by scientific and technical progress became apparent again at the beginning of the twentieth century. It had never been very far from the minds of the poor and the unemployed, but the middle class and the intellectuals had suppressed it. Now, once more, it pervaded literature and philosophy and even began to be suggested in advertising, as on the cover of *Science for Everyone.*

People began to doubt that science held the key to all mysteries; those mysteries only became more numerous as scientific knowledge advanced. Certainty was replaced by probability, objectivity by relativity. Science restricted itself to classifying and to establishing relationships. Some intellectuals, like French critic Ferdinand Brunetière, proclaimed the "failure of science." Others

took up Far Eastern philosophy; rejecting mechanization, violence, and scientism, they followed instead the teachings of Sir Rabindranath Tagore, the Hindu poet, or the Japanese Hasegawa Futabatei, who criticized the notion of progress as conceived by Westerners.

At the same time there was a revival of interest in spiritualism and religion. For some religion simply meant a return to the traditional faith; for others it meant involvement with fanatical or mysterious sects. But mystery and ritual could also be found outside religion. The popularity of Freemasonry, for example, testified to man's desire to find himself in an environment of mystical rites. While not a religion, Freemasonry was involved in religious as well as social and political issues: particularly in France and Italy, it brought together those who wished to reduce the political power of the Catholic Church. The success of Freemasonry was due in large part to man's need to become part of a group, a fraternity. The Freemasons felt that they were "brothers," part of an order that could respond in the modern world to the need for human contact.

The world economy—whose state often subliminally determines behavior and influences ideas—appeared to thrive on the one hand and to be full of difficulties, uncertainties, and misfortunes on the other. An unquestionable economic expansion had taken place since 1895. The worldwide index of industrial productivity rose from 100 in 1899 to 175.7 in 1914. Coal production increased two and a half times; iron production one and a half times; cast-iron production three and a half times. Migration to the cities had not slowed the growth of agricultural production: in the United States, three times more wheat was harvested in 1914 than in 1890.

The rise in national revenues and the doubling of international trade between 1910 and 1913 (it had already doubled between 1870 and 1910) contributed to a higher standard of living. The consumption of food increased: Europe, which had bought one and a half million tons of sugar

Opposite and below: poster by Aldo Mazza for Science for Everyone, a serial publication of Sonzogno of Milan, 1909. Signed at top right. Treviso, Museo Civico Luigi Bailo, Salce Collection.

This famous poster by Gustave Klimt of Theseus and the Minotaur advertised a show by the Secession Academy in their Vienna gallery in 1898. Theseus' nakedness in the original version had offended the censors, so Klimt drew in a tree. Darmstadt, Hessisches Landesmuseum.

Poster by Hjörtzberger for the 1912 Olympics at Stockholm. Signed and dated 1911 at top left. Printed by A. Börtzells, Stockholm. Stuttgart, Staatsgalerie.

in 1898, consumed six million tons in 1913. Meat, milk, and fish appeared more frequently on dining tables, indicating not just a higher standard of living but also a different one. Naturally, not all countries developed at the same rate. Southern and Eastern Europe and the African, Asian, and Latin American colonies lagged. And the "frenzy which makes everyone always produce more and more," as the fiercely protectionist French Prime Minister Félix Jules Méline put it, only exacerbated economic rivalries.

On the other side of the coin, economic

development was interrupted by periodic crises, which produced apprehension, unemployment, and strikes and pitted economically competitive nations even more violently against one another in the search for markets. One critical and recurring problem, overproduction, affected the world economy in 1900–1901, in 1907, and again in 1912–13. Since these crises occurred at a time when prices were rising, they did not stop economic expansion; but they did leave bankruptcies and fear in their wake.

Many socialists predicted that efforts to control overproduction and economic crises would end in an arms race and ultimately in war. "Capitalism carries war as a cloud carries a thunderstorm," warned French socialist Jean Léon Jaurès. The Russo-Japanese War of 1904–5, the Balkan wars, and the expeditions to colonize Africa made clear that warnings of the risks of conflict were not just propaganda or the talk

Poster by Carloz Schwabe for an exhibition at the Durand-Ruel Gallery in Paris, 1892. Signed and dated at lower right. Printed by Draeger et Lesieur, Paris. Stuttgart, Staatsgalerie.

of alarmists. Governments themselves were aware of a relationship between their aggressive foreign policies and social problems at home. In his memoirs, Italian prime minister Giovanni Giolitti explained the motives behind the Italian expedition in Ethiopia. He wrote that in 1893, "public opinion was upset by banking scandals and the governing classes were appalled by the growing socialist agitation; a colonial expedition seemed a welcome diversion."

And in fact, relations among the arms industry, governments, and the military had grown closer. There could be no doubt that the means of destruction had become more plentiful. Rifles and machine guns were being perfected. New explosives like nitroglycerin and smokeless powder were added to the arsenal. New steels permitted the manufacture of bullets and shells with better penetration, as well as armor plating better able to resist them. Swift armor-plated ships were developed in response to the torpedo; the submarine was developed for use against the armored ship.

But the arms race was a heavy burden for national budgets; to a certain degree it was responsible for inflation; and certainly it encouraged militarism. Martial propaganda, the fascination with blood and death, and military confrontations swept Europeans—particularly the young—along. Given the political climate at the beginning of the century, sports and scouting served to intensify the craving for orders, weapons, and regiments. Governments often encouraged the taste for uniforms and parades. In French garrison towns on Saturdays, military bands gave concerts and marched through the streets.

The revived Olympics were not so much peaceful games, in which athletes were moved solely by the sporting spirit, as the symbol of rivalry between nations. On con-

Above: anonymous poster advertising Lake Como as a tourist attraction, about 1900. Treviso, Museo Civico Luigi Bailo. Salce Collection.
Below: poster by Alphonse M. Mucha, about 1898. Signed in the drawing. Paris, Musée des Arts Décoratifs.

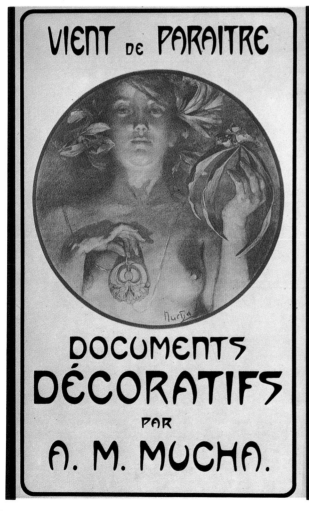

temporary posters for the Olympics or other sports events, young men resembling warriors from antiquity prepared for battle. One poster advertising the opening of the Berlin stadium on June 8, 1913, showed a young athlete who was already the image of the Aryan soldier who would appear, twenty years later, in so many Nazi propaganda posters, statues, and parades. One year before the beginning of World War I, a psychological climate had been established in which fascination with power, virility, violence, and therefore war, flourished.

During the first years of the twentieth century, the Far East unquestionably exerted the strongest outside influence on the arts of Western Europe. Posters, whether they announced an art nouveau exhibition or advertised Lake Como by moonlight, recalled Japanese or Hindu art by their use of stylized flowers and simple lines. In one poster advertising a Rose-Croix exhibition, not only the type face but the representation of the garden seems Far Eastern.

At a time when established values seemed insufficient and people were looking elsewhere, to other cultures, for answers, romanticism was a prevailing popular mood. It rejected the control of reason over passion and stressed that people could be carried away by their sentiments. As a reflection of this attitude, posters whose aim was to sell products showed women posing in attitudes of abandon or gazing up passionately at their lovers.

But while they were being portrayed as dominated by men and by their own emotions, women were continuing to fight for equal rights. In fact there had been a movement for women's emancipation since 1848 in the United States, when women involved in the fight for the abolition of slavery had discovered that they were excluded from debates and political action, particularly voting. As a result the women's movement had been formed at the world's first Women's Rights Convention, held at Seneca Falls, New York, on July 19 and 20, 1848. Other such conventions took place in succeed- **107**

Opposite: detail of a poster by Marcello Dudovich for the aperitif Campari, about 1900. Treviso, Museo Civico Luigi Bailo, Salce Collection.

Bottom right: detail of a poster by Leopoldo Metlicovitz for the Viennese operetta Ein Walzertraum, *1910. Milan, Bertarelli Collection.*

ing years, and about 1860 the movement reached England.

In 1851 the Earl of Carlyle presented a petition in Parliament demanding the vote for women. In 1869 the English philosopher John Stuart Mill's book *The Subjection of Women* called for an end to what he felt was the enslavement of women. In 1883 Susan B. Anthony founded the international feminist movement.

The new woman of the turn of the century became a literary and political topic, particularly in Anglo-Saxon countries. She was shown in posters with a bold expression, her feet up, cigarette in hand. The new woman was a product of economic and social developments.

Women were already at work in the textile factories of northwestern Europe, in English mines, and in metal workshops. Paid less than men, they pulled wagons in the mines, or stood on their feet fifteen hours a day in heavy humid heat washing, or worked in the foundries. The woman's new role in industry changed the traditional relationship between a married woman and her household. It also subjected women to the same economic exploitation as men, and in that sense made them potentially

Above and top right: anonymous British political poster, about 1900. London, Fawcett Library.

men's equals—in abuse if not in salary.

Women were also entering the field of higher education. In the United States and in England during the 1870's, a number of schools for women were established, and their graduates often became militantly active in the feminist movement.

At the same time urban society, the demands of the marketplace, and the growing influence of fashion made women the focus of publicity campaigns. Women constituted the largest market for textiles, household goods, and children's products. Depicting women in advertisements was also an effective way to sell products as diverse as electric lights and typewriters.

The changes that were taking place in society and the pressures of the marketplace could only be favorable to women's emancipation. Their freedom of choice and

therefore their commercial importance had been established, even if at first it applied only to household goods and clothes. Women were gradually becoming liberated from men's tutelage, and their traditional relationship to men was being thrown into question by the changing structure of society itself.

Naturally such a situation had to have political implications. The workers' parties and the unions favored the feminist claims, if perhaps not the most radical ones. There were no doubt cases in factories or workshops where workers, fearing the competition, were happy to see women given only menial jobs. There were also cases where men felt that any jobs available during a time of unemployment should be offered first to them. But despite these reservations the workers' movement increasingly proclaimed

Below: poster by Emily J. Harding for the Artists Suffrage League, about 1900. Signed at lower left. Printed by J. Weiner. London, Fawcett Library.

the necessity of equality between men and women. A few women—such as Rosa Luxemburg, the German left-wing socialist—even played leadership roles in socialist parties.

But the strongest forces for women's full emancipation—including the right to vote—were the freedom of dress and behavior they had achieved in the cities and in their jobs in offices and factories; and their recently established right to an education.

The movement for women's suffrage became particularly strong in Anglo-Saxon countries. In England from 1905 onward, posters, petitions, and meetings multiplied. One poster asked how one could refuse to allow a woman with a university diploma to vote when only convicts and lunatics were barred from the polls. Mrs. Emmeline Pankhurst's Women's Social and Political Union organized numerous demonstrations and practiced civil disobedience. Its members threw stones at Prime Minister Herbert Asquith and attacked the police; one of them threw herself under the king's horse at the Derby. Suffragettes were making headlines.

Of course the greater part of the feminist movement was composed of middle-class women and women with university degrees. Obviously too, many other women were content to be submissive. But the important thing was the developing contrast between the submissive, romantic woman portrayed on some advertising posters and the woman of other posters: the serious university student claiming her right to vote, or the solid barefoot woman brandishing a huge banner of revolt.

Contributing to the liberation of women were technical developments that freed them from many heavy household chores. A revolution that was to have a great impact on everyday habits was under way. The use of gas, for instance, completely changed everyday life, not only because it brought light into the cities and lengthened the day, but because it freed women from having to carry wood or coal. Physical work for both

111

Detail of a poster by Ernst Deutsch for Mercedes typewriters, about 1911. Stuttgart, Staatsgalerie.

Detail of a small poster by Otto Kopp for a study program of German peasant art, 1908. Signed at lower left. Printed by Wolf und Sohn, Munich. Darmstadt, Hessisches Landesmuseum.

German political poster by Karl Maria Stadler published on the occasion of the international Women's Day, March 8, 1914, to advocate women's suffrage. Signed at lower left. Printed by R. Schumann, Munich. Private collection.

women and men was reduced. Women gained hours of free time for themselves, time to improve their minds, and time for their children.

Of course progress was slow. Gas was only gradually being installed in the cities and in people's houses, and the revolution that electricity was to cause had just begun. In 1914 coal still supplied 90 per cent of all energy, with gasoline and gas supplying 7 per cent, and hydraulic power less than 3 per cent. Yet electricity was already being used in industry; in fact it was responsible for the second industrial revolution, which marked the years from 1880 to 1920.

Beginning in the 1830's, when English scientist Michael Faraday invented an electric generator, a series of discoveries established the practical large-scale uses of electricity. In 1871 Belgian electrician Zénobe Gramme displayed the first industrial dynamo at the Academy of Science in Paris. The machine could produce power to light lamps or to run machines; it was versatile, silent, clean, and easy to transport.

At the same time, turbines were developed that made it possible to produce electricity by converting the enormous force of natural waterfalls, such as those in the Alps. In 1891 the city of Frankfurt, Germany, received electricity generated along the Neckar River, 80 miles away, with transformers converting the 15,000-volt current for home use. Steam turbines—with coal providing the steam—became the source of power for generators that provided most of the electricity used industrially and in the home.

Catalonia in Spain and countries like Italy and Switzerland, which have no coal, had not been able to participate in the first industrial revolution, which was built around coal. Electricity changed that, as gradually the alpine landscape became dotted with hydroelectric plants and dams. Across Europe cottage industries and the work of craftsmen were revolutionized by the advent of electricity.

In 1878 Thomas Edison patented the first phonograph. The next year he made a commercially practical incandescent lamp, in which a carbon filament was surrounded by a vacuum inside a glass globe. It brought

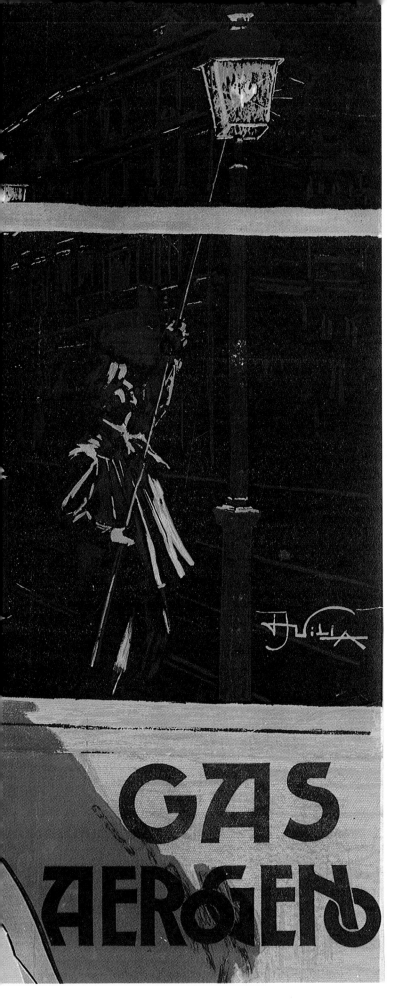

Detail of a poster by Aleardo Villa advertising gas light and heat, about 1900. Signed at right. Printed by Tensi, Milan. Treviso, Museo Civico Luigi Bailo, Salce Collection.

him a fortune, and it gave the world tangible proof of the revolution electricity would cause. Gas lighting was dangerous and smelly and required daily maintenance. Electricity was simplicity itself: with the mere flick of a switch, night could be banished. Posters advertising the sale of light bulbs suggested the vast commercial potential of this new invention.

Electricity was used to drive motors. From 1900 onward subways revolutionized public transport in London, Paris, Berlin, and New York. As travel time became shorter, time for work and leisure increased; and as travel became more comfortable, the physical size of cities increased.

Through electrolysis new metals were developed, such as aluminum, which was malleable and did not oxidize. Among its many applications, aluminum was used to produce lightweight products, such as cooking utensils, which made work easier.

Working conditions in factories were transformed when electric motors began to be used to operate machines, leading to the disappearance of the long belts and pulleys characteristic of steam propulsion. Factory work became quieter, cleaner, safer, and less exhausting. Electricity was indeed affecting many different aspects of people's lives.

There was now a constant intercommunication between science, technology, and daily life. Electricity found practical application while scientists were still investigating its nature. X-rays were used in medicine very soon after their discovery. The simplest aspects of daily life began to be affected by progress in the application of technology.

Studies of the properties of electricity did more than change everyday life. In fact science was entering areas far removed from man's everyday experience, and new discoveries were shaking the traditional principles on which physics had been based.

Experiments with electricity led in turn to the discovery of radiation and the subatomic structure of matter. In 1895 Wilhelm Roentgen discovered that electrical cathode **115** rays emitted penetrating rays, which he called x-rays. Then in 1897 Englishman Joseph John Thomson discovered that these cathode rays were negative electric particles, or electrons, which were much smaller than the smallest known atom. Scientists soon realized that all atoms contained electrons and other, positive particles called protons. The theory that the atom was the smallest particle in the universe had been shattered.

In 1896 French scientist Antoine Henri Becquerel discovered in uranium the property of radioactivity—that is, the spontaneous emission of electrons and other particles. Pierre and Marie Curie continued Becquerel's work in radioactivity and in 1898 discovered the radioactive element radium. Their work cast doubt on the idea that there was a clear distinction between matter and energy.

The theory that matter and energy were separate was put finally to rest with the formulation of two theories: Albert Einstein's special theory of relativity (1905), which held that space and time were not absolute but relative; and Max Planck's quantum theory (beginning in 1901), which held that matter emits energy in discontinuous packets, or quanta, rather than continuously, as had been previously thought.

By 1913, too, Ernest Rutherford and Niels Bohr had constructed a model of the atom. The result of all these discoveries was that the previously accepted concept of the objective reality of nature—in which all natural phenomena were theoretically understandable and even predictable—was destroyed. The idea of one objective reality was replaced with that of many subjective realities; determinism was replaced by statistical probability.

Despite antagonisms of growing virulence, nations and individuals were in one sense drawing closer together thanks to improved means of communication.

Guglielmo Marconi, Sir Oliver Lodge, and Édouard Branly all contributed to the development of the wireless telegraph. Marconi perfected the transmission of electromagnetic waves; in 1899 he sent the first telegraph between England and France, and in 1901 he received the first transatlantic signals. Early in the twentieth century Sir John Ambrose Fleming invented, and Lee De Forest improved, the electron tube, thus opening the frontiers of radio. With Edwin H. Armstrong's 1912 invention of a regenerative circuit, long-distance radio reception became feasible.

The early part of the twentieth century saw the rapid development and growing popularity of movies. The age of motion pictures was really introduced in 1889, when Thomas Edison developed the Kinetograph, a camera that used rolls of film, and the

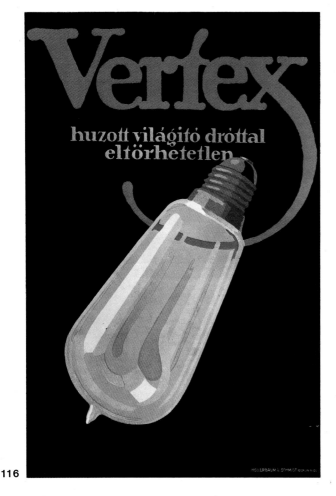

huzott világító dróttal eltörhetetlen

CINÉMATOGRAPHE

Kinetoscope, a peepshowlike device for viewing the films. In 1895 the French brothers Auguste and Louis Lumière created the Cinématographe, an adaption of the Kinetoscope that enabled images to be projected on a screen. The Lumière brothers presented a public showing of their famous early film sequence *L'Arroseur arrosé* (The waterer watered) at the Grand Café in Paris on December 28, 1895, and again in January, 1896.

From the beginning cinematography was a popular art form. A Pathé advertisement called cinema "entertainment for the humble and the workers." And indeed, soldiers on leave and workers filled the first movie houses. But as the novelty of the earliest efforts wore off, audiences grew restless. The documentaries showing the coronation of Nicholas II or episodes from the Russo-Japanese War of 1905 no longer attracted crowds. These films were too short and amateurish to have any long-range appeal, and for a while it seemed as if movies would become only a technical curiosity.

At this point, however, Frenchman George Méliés abandoned the technique of recording real-life scenes in a straightforward manner. Instead he became the first to tell a story, using a series of photographic tricks to help make the setting seem realistic. Méliés' great accomplishments, *Cinderella* (1900) and his 1902 film *Le Voyage dans la Lune* (A trip to the moon), were copied and reproduced in America. After Edwin S. Porter introduced the technique of editing in *The Great Train Robbery* (1903)—a procedure that enabled the continuity of shots to become important—a new era of movie making began. By 1914 Hollywood had become movie capital of the United States, the first feature-length film had been made in Europe, and the era of lavish productions had been inaugurated with the Italian movie *Quo Vadis* (1913).

Thanks to movies, people became very much visually oriented at the beginning of the twentieth century. Posters, which were becoming increasingly popular as a means of advertising, had already come to rely on

design and colors rather than words to communicate their message. Films accentuated this evolution toward efforts to create immediate visual impact.

Movies were not, however, immediately popular with all levels of society. Not until November 17, 1908, did the Paris newspaper *Le Temps* print a review of a film, *The Assassination of the Duke of Guise.* It did so then only because the stars were members of the Comédie Française and because all the best people in Paris had gone to see it. In general, the cinema remained an art for the masses. The elite preferred the theater and books.

This cultural fragmentation occurred all over Europe, but particularly in some of the oldest and most centralized countries, such 120 as France, Italy—with its antagonism be-

tween north and south—Germany, and the Austro-Hungarian Empire. Groups, classes, and regions strongly maintained their individuality, and even the influence of nationalism in the second half of the nineteenth century had not resulted in complete integration. The various social groups often found themselves set against one another because of their different tastes, ways of life, and cultures.

Politics was more important to the masses than cultural preoccupations; yet their participation in politics was extremely limited, aside from the important ritual of casting their votes. Unions and socialist parties were able to organize only limited numbers of people from those classes of society that should have been concerned with political action. Such important questions as the Dreyfus affair often interested

GABRIELE D'ANNUNZIO

OFF. G. RICORDI e C. MILANO

CABIRIA

only politically aware people and intellectuals. The masses became involved only during strikes or uprisings, such as Bloody Week in Italy in 1914 or the social trouble that occurred in France between 1907 and 1910.

On the other hand, nationalistic feelings and patriotism were the strongest factors working toward integration and a leveling of the differences between the classes. This was certainly true in an ancient country like France; less so in Italy.

The twentieth century was marked by speed. Telegrams and radio transmitted information instantaneously. Electricity lighted up a room at the touch of a switch. And for relatively rapid transportation, there was the automobile.

During its first years, the expensive, dashing automobile was a plaything of the social elite. Cars driven by chauffeurs with impressive caps carried women wrapped in sumptuous furs. The automobile was still surrounded with mystery. The driver and his passenger were bold explorers of a new world.

From the beginning each make of car had its own unique features. Ford offered a *voiturette*, a little car, elegant and light like the woman driving it. The Mercedes had nobler pretentions, as suggested by the poster showing several in front of a columned palace. In an austere Opel poster, the driver has the dignity of a military man of high rank, yet his strange, piercing look seems to invite the viewer toward the unknown.

As these posters suggest, brand names were very quickly substituted for the word "automobile." Dominating the posters were the words "Ford," "Mercedes," "Opel," in large letters. An owner began to refer to his automobile not as "a car made by Ford" but simply as "a Ford." Opel, Ford, Renault, Fiat, Citroën became not just familiar names but, because of their use on posters, symbols of power, or wealth, or speed. The day of the automobile—with its emblems and trade names, its elegant passengers and

drivers with turned-up collars and goggles—had arrived.

All this had become possible because in several industries important discoveries had resulted in new products and improved production methods. Among the new products were special steels that were both malleable and strong enough to be used in the manufacture of car parts. They contained nickel, chrome, and tungsten and were most easily created in the electric furnace.

Industrial and technical progress produces chain reactions: a discovery, or the use of a new source of energy, has many consequences. Car assembly was facilitated by oxyacetylene welding, which in turn had become possible through the discovery of acetylene; and that in turn had been obtained from calcium carbine produced in electric furnaces.

The modern automobile was made possible by the development of the internal-combustion engine. In the 1880's German engineer Gottlieb Daimler made significant improvements in this engine, and in 1885 Karl Benz built the first car powered by an internal-combustion engine. Its top speed was twelve miles an hour.

The 1890's saw the rapid development of the automobile. Refinements in motor design in 1891 made cars capable of higher speeds. A top was added to the passenger compartment so that passengers could ride 123

comfortably in any weather; the driver, however, was still at the mercy of the elements, like the coachman he had replaced. But with higher speeds possible, designers soon began to streamline the car body and put a roof over the front seat. Improvements in the suspension and the addition of shock absorbers made longer trips possible.

On the eve of World War I cars were capable of going fifty miles an hour, and rallies and races were organized. People were enthusiastic about automobiles, which soon became a familiar sight. They were the symbols of all that was modern and forward looking. In 1914 there were two million cars in existence: one million in the United States, the rest in Europe. Cars were especially prevalent in the industrially developed countries, and in turn they helped speed that development.

In fact cars created a whole industry. The factories where they were made used the most advanced production methods: Ford automobiles, for instance, were mass produced on production lines. The internal-combustion engine created a market for petroleum, which until then had been used—in limited quantity—mostly for lighting. (It had also been used in the boilers of some ships, notably Napoleon III's yacht.) The automobile industry needed steel and textiles, and it also needed rubber for tires. As the demand for rubber grew, the establishment of rubber plantations changed the landscape of Southeast Asia. A world economy had become a reality.

While rubber plantations changed the Asian landscape, the growing number of automobiles changed the landscape of the developed countries. Before the arrival of the train and the automobile, there had not

been much difference between urban and rural means of transportation. At first cars were driven on dirt roads, leaving clouds of dust behind them; to protect themselves, drivers had to wear goggles and women passengers large hats held down by veils. Eventually roads began to be covered with tar, a new product produced from the destructive distillation of coal. Roads became black bands snaking their way through the fields; they were no longer part of the countryside. They connected cities, and the cars that passed over them helped close the gap between city and country.

In the sky, too, new machines were beginning to appear. At first there were airships—power-driven balloons with directional controls. The first of these appeared in 1852. In 1900 Count Ferdinand von Zeppelin developed the rigid airship named after him. Soon zeppelins were carrying passengers and traveling more than thirty miles per hour.

But the real milestone in flight came in 1903, when Orville and Wilbur Wright for the first time flew a winged, heavier-than-air craft. From then on the balloon took a back seat to the airplane. In 1909 Louis Blériot flew across the English Channel in 26 minutes. Planes crossed the Alps and the

126

Mediterranean. By 1914 a plane had traveled as fast as 120 miles an hour, at a maximum altitude of 18,000 feet, covering a distance of 600 miles. In a very few years, aviation had come of age.

To see man fly, mastering machine and speed, to see streets bursting with automobile traffic and stores offering such a variety of goods for sale, one might have thought that by 1914 the twentieth century had accomplished as much as it could. Yet in 1914 the urban islands where twentieth-century innovations had effected dramatic changes were surrounded by vast spaces where not much had changed since the middle of the nineteenth century. Unsettling changes had not yet come to central Europe, Russia, and some of the regions around the Mediterranean. Capitalism had not yet been challenged by the socialist economic and political system, as it would be later in the century.

Although by 1914 the world was divided by rivalries and conflicts, it nevertheless had been drawn closer together through improved methods of distributing information, merchandise, and ideas. In the developed countries even people's habits had become similar, so that, for example, in two different countries, posters with similar themes would be used to advertise similar products.

Influenced by an abundant production of goods, people began to aspire to a longer and happier life. Further, the diversity of goods and pleasures in the cities was enough to make city dwellers wonder why they should work so hard. This question could never be asked in the country, where everything depended on the harvest and therefore on labor.

Of course in the city the products offered for sale had to be paid for. Perhaps the end of the direct link between production and consumption caused some of the apprehension that seemed to pervade the belle époque. In any event, while products were available, and advertising whetted appetites for them, many still could not afford them.

Socialist parties promised the working-man the end of injustice, the abolition of money, and an equal share of wealth. Yet at the same time economic necessities, nationalist feelings, and the self-interests of autocracies fearful of further revolts were priming the world for war. It would soon become clear that production techniques could be used for the destruction of people and property as well as to make life better and more comfortable.

Heads of government seemed quite willing to commit themselves to the miseries of war. "War is inevitable," said Georges Clemenceau in 1908, and Theodore Roosevelt proclaimed in a style that anticipated the ideologies of the twentieth century: "Only war will allow us to acquire the virile qualities necessary to be victorious in the merciless battle which these times impose."

The futurists—an early-twentieth-century 127

Konkurrenz-Fliegen
der erßen Aviatiker der Welt
26. September – 3. Oktober 1909
Flugplatz Berlin-Johannisthal
150,000 Mk. Geldpreiſe
Deutſche Flugplatz-Geſellſchaft ✱
Billets: A. Werfheim ✱ Invalidendank

school of Italian artists who glorified war, machines, and danger, and in doing so helped create a climate favorable to fascism—went even further. F. T. Marinetti, a futurist leader, wrote: "We want to glorify militarism, patriotism, the destructiveness of the anarchists' murderous ideologies, and the contempt of women." And Gabriele D'Annunzio, an early supporter of fascism, stirred Italy with his "Chosen nation, may you one day see the banks of the Mediterranean drenched with blood in your war."

An explosive mixture of economic imperatives, social antagonisms, and new ideologies was brewing all over Europe. It was as if a whole civilization watched the approach of war with fascination; as if people, swept away by the propaganda, had already accepted the coming holocaust without a thought of the consequences. At the First

Hague Peace Conference in 1899 Kaiser Wilhelm II had declared: "I will play in this comedy of a conference but I will keep my sword at my side for the waltz." The waltz was about to begin.

Besides Europe and the already industrialized United States, there were other worlds in ferment. Asia was powerful and seething: Japan had crushed Russia, and China had become a republic in 1911. Islam was defeated but not subdued. Africa had been brought into contact with the rest of the world by its colonizers and so had been opened to the dream of emancipation. In 1914, when the first shots were fired, the world seemed ready for war.

Soon posters selling the latest fashions were replaced by posters calling for sacrifice and blood and heroism. For four years the theme of war was dominant.

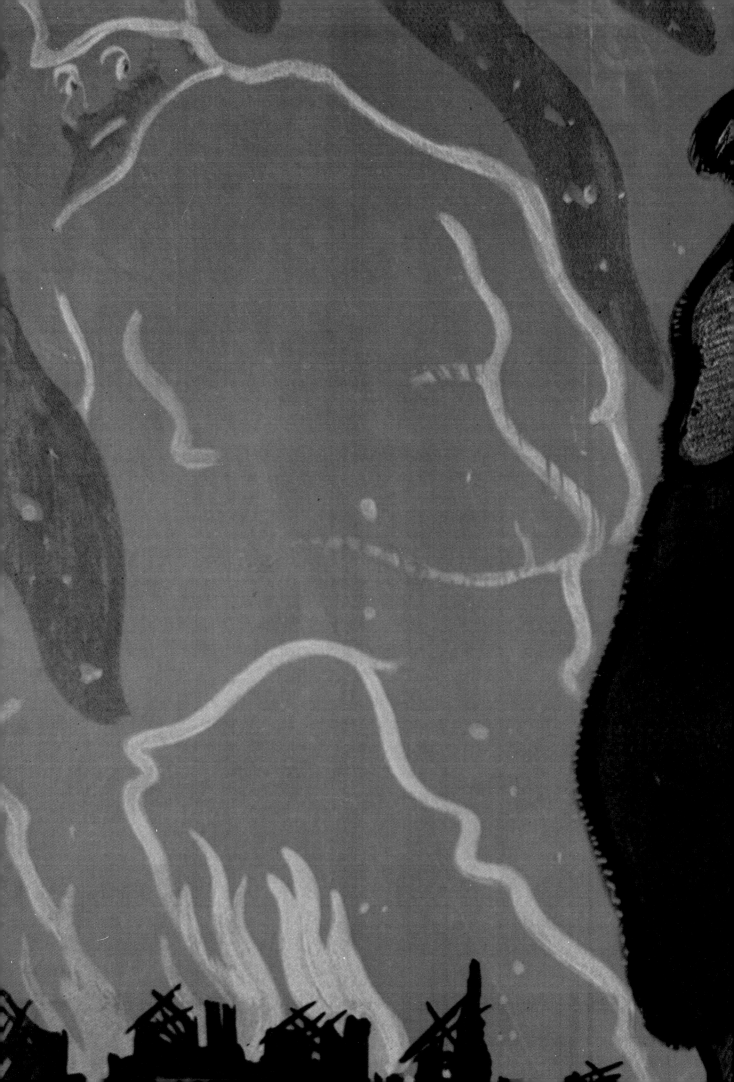

1914–1924
Images of War
and Revolution

The war people had feared—but had not really believed would come—engulfed Europe. It was set off by Serbian nationalist Gavrilo Princip's assassination of Austrian Archduke Francis Ferdinand at Sarajevo on June 28, 1914.

The assassination itself might not have led to war had it not been for those other tensions—economic competition, imperialist ambitions, ardent nationalism—that had been building over the previous decades. The major European powers already were split into two defensive alliances, the Triple Alliance and the Triple Entente. An arms race had been escalating dangerously for years. French nationalists hated Germany for forcing France to cede Alsace-Lorraine after the humiliating defeat in the Franco-Prussian War. German nationalists gloried in their country's new unity. Dissatisfied Slavic minorities agitating for freedom posed a grave threat to the Austro-Hungarian Empire. Meanwhile European powers were struggling with one another for economic superiority, as well as for dominant influence in Africa and Asia.

Yet, as we have already seen, still other factors lulled many into a false sense of security. Industrialization had produced unparalleled prosperity. Communications between nations were increasing, thanks to electronic advances. Culturally too, countries were growing closer together. War seemed impossible in so civilized a world.

Nonetheless, with the assassination at Sarajevo events moved Europe inexorably to war. Austria-Hungary, determined to punish Serbia, presented that country with a totally unacceptable ultimatum, then on July 28 declared war. Russia, Serbia's ally, immediately mobilized; Germany in turn declared war on Russia; and in rapid order France, Belgium, and Great Britain joined Russia against Germany and Austria. Japan soon entered on the side of the Allies (Russia, Great Britain, France, Belgium), while the Ottoman Empire joined the Central Powers. In 1915 Italy joined the Allies. By the time the United States entered in 1917, the war was truly worldwide.

131

Illustration from a Hungarian poster by Biró urging the reconstruction of the destroyed village of Saros, about 1915–16. Signed at lower right. Printed by Frankun Tarsulat, Budapest. Paris, Musée de la Guerre.

Below and far left on page 133: poster by James Montgomery Flagg for the U.S. army, 1917. Signed at right. New York, Museum of Modern Art.

Below and second from left on page 133: poster by Achille Luciano Mauzan for a national war loan in Italy, 1917. Signed at top right. Printed by Butteri, Turin. Treviso, Museo Civico Luigi Bailo, Salce Collection.

Bottom and second from right on page 133: anonymous German enlistment poster, about 1915-16. Stuttgart, Staatsgalerie.

When the war ended, Europe had been devastated, with thousands of its villages in ruins, millions of its people left homeless, hundreds of thousands of its young men lost in a mindless war of attrition. The poster showing an anguished woman outside her destroyed village captures the horror that the war embodied for so many.

Europe lost her supremacy in the First World War. Too many died: 1,357,800 in France, 1,773,700 in Germany, 1,700,000 in Russia, 908,371 in the United Kingdom, 650,000 in Italy. In addition to those killed in battle, the mortality rate at home almost tripled between 1914 and 1918, while the birth rate decreased by 45 per cent. The war also left millions of cripples and millions of veterans who were to influence their nations' political futures on the grounds that the war had given them moral "rights."

Added to the wreckage of men and money was that of property. Mines and factories were destroyed in the occupied countries, and both victors and vanquished were burdened with war debts.

It was a new type of war. The total of several million men assembled on the battlefield came from all levels of society, although peasants made up the majority. In addition, colonial regiments were recruited from all over the world.

Manpower was also needed behind the lines, in factories. During the autumn of 1914, after the Germans had advanced to the Marne River, the front settled down. It was understood in Paris, London, and Berlin that this war would be long, and that its outcome would depend not only on armies but above all on weapons, which in turn depended on economic mobilization, the conversion of factories to the manufacture of armaments. Governments were asked to take over industries. In this way the war led to a form of state control that would become characteristic of the twentieth century.

133

Left and below: Australian recruitment poster by B. E. Pike, 1914–15. Signed at lower right. Canberra, Australian War Memorial.

Anonymous recruitment poster, 1914. Printed in Dublin by Hely's. London, Imperial War Museum.

The war revealed that the values of nineteenth-century society and civilization had failed to protect the world from self-destruction. One result was that after the war the countries that fought became susceptible to new ideologies ranging from fascism to communism.

The problems of our epoch were forged in World War I.

The poster played an important role in wartime. In some countries it was used to persuade men to join the army. During the first years of the war, for instance, Britain did not impose conscription. Until 1916 the government tried through posters and other propaganda to persuade Englishmen to enlist by appealing to their pride or their sense of duty. But most of the warring countries raised armies through universal military conscription; so eventually did Britain and the United States. Persuading men to enlist, then, was not a principal function of posters. What many people had to be persuaded of was the need for total commitment and effort. Factories at home had to be manned. Supplies had to be conserved.

Most important, morale had to be maintained. These were selling jobs for which posters were well suited.

The traditional presuffragette relationship between men and women was reestablished in wartime, at least so far as posters were concerned. Men were confronted with the argument that their women wanted them to go to war. Women were presented as strong-willed, determined, but essentially in need of protection. War posters made use of traditional family relationships. Many of them show children clinging to their dignified, courageous, beautiful mothers. It was imperative to unify society so that it could focus its efforts, and for this reason much of the war propaganda emphasized men's traditional role of defending family and home against the enemy.

It is interesting to note, in many posters, that the appeal was presented in terms of defending one's family rather than one's country. This is not to suggest, however, that appeals to patriotism were not pervasive in the efforts to arouse people. Indeed, propaganda linked the defense of personal property with the defense of country. In a sense the World War I soldier was exhorted to fight for a fatherland personified by his family. One reason for this technique was that the armies confronting each other were no longer made up of mercenaries but of conscripts from all levels of society. These nonprofessional soldiers had to be given a personal, immediate reason for fighting.

Another psychological technique used in posters was an effort to make every individual feel that he was being appealed to personally and to make each one feel guilty if he did not sign up and help. All countries used this approach. In American, German, French, and Italian posters, fingers pointed at passers-by. Other posters reminded those on the home front not to forget the fighting men: soldiers stare out with intense, fixed eyes, intimidating the citizen who has not yet committed himself enough to the war effort or who has not yet made his contribution toward the "victory loan."

The longer the war lasted the more civilian life had to be organized. Behind the lines life had to go on. It was a difficult life; food was rationed, and often the poor were hungry. The incomes of many could not keep up with rising prices. Women were working in factories, and salaries had increased, but the scarcity of some products and the black-market dealing in others, as well as the privations brought on by the lack of certain basic products such as coal, severely reduced standards of living.

As the war ground on, demanding increasingly more, rations had to be reduced everywhere. In Germany in 1918 people had only four ounces of flour, half an ounce of meat, and a quarter of an ounce of fat a day. In Russia too, shortages were severe. France, the United Kingdom, Italy, and the neutral countries felt the pinch of rationing to a lesser degree. One effect of the restrictions imposed on basic necessities such as coal, oil, sugar, meat, antiseptics, and soap was an upsurge of epidemics, virus infections, and the "Spanish flu," which broke out during the last months of the war.

The difficulties of life on the home front contrasted sharply with the easy life of war profiteers. Certain industrialists, middlemen, and salesmen not only prospered hugely but were able to avoid going to the front because of their "special position." This was one reason why posters appealing to each citizen's conscience gradually lost their effectiveness as the war continued. **135**

Below and bottom left: poster by Théophile Steinlen advertising tickets for a raffle to aid starving Belgians, about 1918. Paris, Musée des Arts Décoratifs.

Below and bottom right: poster by G. Greppi for the regional mobilization committee of Lombardy, about 1917. Milan, Museo del Risorgimento.

The ostentatiously easy life many people led seemed scandalous to the poor and to those whose relatives were fighting in the front lines.

One result of this disillusionment was that gradually the "sacred union," which in most countries had united the various political factions from socialists to conservatives, disintegrated. Strikes broke out in defense factories. Women organized demonstrations. The socialists left governments in which they had accepted posts in 1914. In

Above center: poster by Illion asking Spaniards to save food, about 1917. Signed at right. Paris, Musée des Arts Décoratifs.

Russia widespread unrest and dissatisfaction culminated in the Russian Revolution of 1917. That revolution in turn gave new impetus to resistance to the war.

With this breach in political unity, these cracks in solidarity, governments found themselves fighting not just war on the fronts but defeatism and even treason at home. As a result propaganda, through speeches and posters, was stepped up. And when the power of the image was not sufficient, the force of the law was applied: traitors were dealt with under martial law or by courts-martial.

A comparison of the patriotic posters and the martial climate of World War I with those of the French Revolution of 1789 vividly illustrates the changes that had occurred. Words, which had been so important in 1789, by World War I had almost disappeared from posters in favor of the suggestive, moving, gripping image. Posters came to rely heavily on immediate visual impact, rather than text, to convey their message. Furthermore, the individual being appealed to was no longer primarily part of a group, governed by a revolutionary popular government. He was isolated and ruled by an all-powerful government that despite its various personifications—Uncle Sam, John Bull—remained completely anonymous. Uncle Sam pointing at each American symbolized the new relationship: the citizen is alone, pursued to the depth of his conscience by the state. The man subjected to this propaganda, these repeated injunctions, these ever-present images, could no longer escape his duty.

War posters used stark images—haggard refugees, pale and hungry children, weeping widows—to convince those who wished to ignore the war of the need for national **137**

Right: American poster by Casper Emerson, Jr., for war bonds, 1917. Paris, Musée des Arts Décoratifs.

Below: detail from a German poster of 1917 by Alfred Offner advertising the seventh war loan. Munich, Neue Staatsgalerie.

solidarity. Italians appealed to their relatives living in the United States to remember them. Posters tried to persuade people to buy less, to eat little, to economize: to do their patriotic duty. But the appeal for unanimity could not mask the presence of forces that refused to comply with the governments' wishes.

The working classes had been temporarily disoriented by the suddenness of war, the assassination of Jean Léon Jaurès, the abrupt about-face of the heads of socialist parties, and the consequent disintegration of the Second International Workingmen's Association. But even while the war continued, contrasts between the classes became pronounced once more.

Internal tensions surfaced first in countries that had no strong nationalistic tradition. In Italy, which had entered the war at the instigation of an active minority of intellectuals and members of the lower middle class, the socialist party all along favored a policy of neutrality and noninter-

vention. The government, in an effort to escape responsibility for military mistakes—especially the crushing defeat of the Italian army by the Austrians at Caporetto in October, 1917—tried to blame the socialists and workers who were staffing the armament factories.

From then on bitterness in Italy spread. One poster graphically suggested the tensions among classes: it shows an indignant soldier, accompanied by weeping widows, exhorting factory employees to join the war effort. The silent workers, hands in their pockets, look indifferent. The contrast is vivid: on the one hand there is the patriotic, disciplined soldier, looking heroic and dependable in his uniform; on the other hand are the workers, so rarely represented on posters, looking hostile and decidedly unmilitary in their rumpled clothes, their scarves, and their shapeless caps and hats. The workers look as if the war holds very little meaning for them; the soldier looks as if it means everything to him.

Poster by Girus exhorting Italians to give money for victory and peace, 1917. Signed è left. Milan, Museo del Risorgimento.

This poster tells us a great deal about the real antagonism and strong feelings that divided the two sides. And it helps explain the confrontations that would take place after the war, as the sides grew steadily farther apart. Many of those who fought or actively supported the war were ardent nationalists who did not want the efforts of their dead comrades to be forgotten, who were committed to bringing glory to their country. Some of them would become fascists or Nazis, exploiting nationalistic ideals for their own purposes. On the other side were those who were not committed to a nationalistic war, who had not given their blood, who even killed returning soldiers; they were considered defeatists and even traitors by some. The goals of social revolution touched them more closely than nationalist ambitions; after the war they would become Communists rather than **140** fascists.

The war, like all wars, devoured money. It was needed to purchase raw materials; it was needed to supply, feed, and pay millions of soldiers. As a result, the state needed not only people's blood but also their money. The appeals to give, to subscribe, never ended.

DEBOUT DANS LA TRANCHÉE
QUE L'AURORE ÉCLAIRE, LE SOLDAT
RÊVE À LA VICTOIRE ET À SON FOYER.
POUR QU'IL PUISSE ASSURER L'UNE
ET RETROUVER L'AUTRE.
SOUSCRIVEZ
AU 3ᵉ EMPRUNT DE LA DÉFENSE NATIONALE

By borrowing, the state mortgaged its future.

During World War I the public debt multiplied seven times in France, eleven times in Britain, six times in Italy, and twenty-seven times in Germany. The colossal cost **142** of that war increased the foreign debts of the various nations proportionally even more. Europe's supremacy was undermined by the fact that it owed the United States billions of gold dollars.

This indebtedness and the insatiable need for money introduced a new element into everyday life: inflation. For centuries money

RED CROSS OR IRON CROSS?

WOUNDED AND A PRISONER
OUR SOLDIER CRIES FOR WATER.
THE GERMAN "SISTER"
POURS IT ON THE GROUND BEFORE HIS EYES.
THERE IS NO WOMAN IN BRITAIN
WHO WOULD DO IT.
THERE IS NO WOMAN IN BRITAIN
WHO WILL FORGET IT.

Left and below: anti-German poster by David Wilson, 1917. Signed at lower right in the drawing. London, Imperial War Museum.

had been stable. Stockholders were envied members of society, for they had invested their money and were able to live year after year on the interest it yielded. From time to time they bought foreign bonds—Russian ones, for instance, since the czarist empire was considered immortal.

Then the war broke out and prices rose. Banknotes were printed by the millions, and shares were no longer worth anything. Hundreds of thousands of small shareholders were ruined. Confidence in the state and in social stability was destroyed. Instability and apprehension swept the middle classes. **143**

Above: German poster by Richard Klein entitled The Day of Sacrifice, *about 1918. Signed at lower left. Printed in Munich by C. Wolf und Sohn. Munich, Haus der Kunst.*

The groups most affected by this monetary erosion began to envy salaried people, who managed to cope despite the war because their salaries were raised to keep pace with rising prices. The resentments that developed were to be very useful to the fascists.

The profoundest influence on the postwar period, and the greatest aid to fascism, was the apprenticeship in violence that millions of men had undergone during the preceding four years. One cannot understand the Fascist or Nazi parades held in Rome and Nuremberg without recognizing the long and dangerous military companionship that many of the participants had lived through during the First World War. Ob-

144 viously not all veterans became fascists or Nazis; but all the Nazi bosses were veterans who had learned to appreciate weapons, risked death and killed, knew the importance of an army, and especially knew how worthless a human life could be, because they had seen so many lost.

The army had created a new man, trained not to think for himself but to follow orders, even if those orders meant an inevitable march to death. All soldiers at one time or another were forced to take part in unnecessary attacks planned solely to enhance the prestige of one or another officer; they all knew that irresponsible staff decisions had caused the death of hundreds or thousands of their comrades. Yet these soldiers, conditioned both by discipline and fear, continued to obey even the most obviously

Far left and below left: German poster by Willy Stöwer asking for contributions to finance submarines, 1917. Stuttgart, Staatsgalerie.

Left and below: American poster by L. A. Shafer, 1917. Signed at bottom. Milan, Museo del Risorgimento.

suicidal orders. The French soldier, for instance, knew he could choose between the "enemy and the police"; that is, he could choose between staying at the front and being shot by the enemy, or retreating and being executed by a firing squad.

The continuing obedience of armies in the face of death and of the evident negligence of many officers persuaded some veterans that masses of men could be molded to do and accept anything. One had only to hold them by fear, isolate them, and strike down without hesitation those who rebelled.

The methods applied by Adolf Hitler and Benito Mussolini owed a large debt to the lessons of the First World War.

The war that had set nations against one another for four years excited intense nationalistic feelings and produced profound resentments—the more so because the battles had been of an intensity and cruelty without precedent. Life in the cold, muddy trenches was punctuated by bombardments that buried men alive or by frequent assaults with fixed bayonets that ended in hand-to-hand combat. Sometimes in the middle of a battle gas rolled along the trenches, blinding men and causing them to panic; then the attack would resume, with an initial assault wave followed by units of "trench cleaners," who would finish off the survivors with hand grenades or side arms.

Each side insisted that it was right, that its army fought with God's help; the German "God be with us" was echoed by the French "May God protect France, the eldest daughter of the church." Propaganda depicted the enemy as the incarnation of evil—at worst murderous and cruel, at best ridiculous. Each country assumed humanity, **145**

Below: poster by G. Caron praising and encouraging the diligence of French women during the war, 1917. Paris, Private collection.

Bottom: illustration from a poster by Edward Penfield entitled Save Wheat, *asking for increased agricultural production to help France, about 1917. Washington, National Library.*

OVERLEAF: *illustration from a French poster of 1918–19 by Faime requesting a loan to "liberate" Alsace from the Germans. The kaiser, his sword broken, bends under the weight of the flags of victorious countries. Paris, Musée des Arts Décoratifs.*

Opposite: anonymous Russian poster advertising a war loan, 1916. London, Imperial War Museum.

LA FEMME FRANÇAISE PENDANT LA GUERRE

SECTION CINÉMATOGRAPHIQUE de l'ARMÉE FRANÇAISE

courage, and glory as national characteristics. Gone was the notion that these values in any way transcended national boundaries.

Posters reinforced this attitude, inciting contempt, hatred, and indignation. In one English poster, a German nurse refuses to give water to a wounded prisoner, pouring it on the ground before the thirsty man's eyes; in the background are caricatures of laughing Prussian officers. Posters rarely showed the horror of battle or the mangled corpses, however. One German poster showing a suffering wounded soldier being helped by his comrades gives the impression of strength, even of tenderness, combined with heroic determination. It fails to present the ugliness and shame of war, showing only a sweetened version of it and its consequences.

In all this propaganda the very real suffering of men was disregarded. That this suffering was experienced and shared by all the combatants explains why those who lived through the hell of the front lines often felt less hatred than those at home, whose idea of war as a confrontation between good and evil was shaped by propaganda.

Meanwhile the great slaughter continued day after day. By the end of 1915 the French army already had lost almost 600,000 men, of whom 16,000 were officers. In 1916 the six-month-long Battle of Verdun cost each side more than 300,000 men; that year more than 2 million soldiers were put out of action on the Western front alone. At the end of the second year of the war, Russia had already lost 3,800,000 men.

If those on the home front did not clearly understand what the war did to soldiers, it was because propaganda both disguised the truth and created its own myths. Legends grew around the submarine and the airplane, the two newest weapons of war. Infantrymen bogged down in mud and blood were not likely to provoke dreams of glory, but the more glamorous submarine captains or airplane pilots could. In the mysterious worlds of the sea and the sky, submarines and airplanes became "wolves" or "eagles,"

moving sleekly and gracefully, dispensing death at a distance. The man at the submarine periscope gave the order to fire, and far away a boat exploded and sank. The fighter pilot was on his own. One did not have to think of the sailors in the sinking ship, drowning in a thick layer of fuel oil, or of the civilians wiped out by the bombs.

Legends grew up around these two new types of warfare partly because they were always presented intellectually as branches of technology rather than as means of destruction and homicide. The fascination of a large part of the population with machinery was thus exploited with regard to the new weapons. The 1914 war opened up new possibilities of technical development. Ironically, the fleets of airplanes that bombarded industrial regions heralded the development of the civilian aircraft industry and introduced the plane to everyday life.

The war also affected women's role in society. At first women appeared in propaganda in their traditional roles as mothers and wives. But very soon, as labor became scarce, women went to work in factories and on farms, working lathes, pulling plows, tilling the fields, and taking in the harvest. In offices they replaced the men who had been mobilized. With their men away from home, women finally discovered that they were in all respects men's equals. Their rights were gradually acknowledged and slowly became law.

For a while after the war the victorious nations, even though exhausted, believed that the prewar good times would return and that it would be possible to eradicate the previous four bloody years. Statesmen and returning soldiers all believed that they had survived the last war. The Allies thought that they had fought for great principles and had won because morality was on their side; their combined strength, symbolized in one poster by national flags, had caused the fall of the German empire. Yet on the other bank of the Rhine, the vanquished were not prepared to admit that right and justice were

Poster by Nikolai Kokhergin for May Day, 1920. Private collection.

the prerogatives only of the victors.

Actually, since 1914 certain radicals had done their utmost to point out that the warring nations were not fighting solely for great principles and that responsibility for the war had to be shared by all the belligerents. Socialists charged that the capitalist system itself was guilty and that the German and French peoples were losing their lives for the benefit of imperialists.

In October, 1917, a Russian socialist revolutionary group, the Bolsheviks, staged an armed coup d'état in Russia, overthrowing the provisional government that had been established following the abdication of the czar several months earlier. Thereafter the Bolshevik menace—or hope, depending on one's point of view—was a political factor throughout Europe.

After the seizure of power by the Bolsheviks (who soon changed their name to the Communist party), civil war wracked Russia for three years as the anti-Bolshevik White Russian army attempted to gain control. Despite foreign intervention—Japanese, French, British, and American troops occupied several Russian cities, ostensibly to keep large Allied stores from falling into German hands—the White Russian forces of Generals Anton Denikin, Pëtr Nikolaevich Wrangel, Nikolai Nikolaevich Yudenich, and Admiral Aleksandr Kolchak were ultimately defeated. Russia was in ruins, but for the first time Communists had successfully taken over a country.

Bolshevism inspired strong passions, whether fear or hope, hatred or enthusiasm. On one side the Bolsheviks were considered no better than pirates with bloody knives or new barbarians. People's fears had changed little since the nineteenth century: the middle class of 1920 was just as fearful of the "Reds" as the middle class of 1848 or 1871 had been.

Communist propaganda was just as exaggerated as that of the other side; one poster shows a gigantic hero of the Red army about to cut off the greedy hand of a czarist partisan, an aristocratic officer of the White army. On both sides messages were simpli-

151

Detail from a Bolshevik poster by D. S. Moore entitled Wrangel Is Alive, Finish Him Off without Pity, *referring to a White Russian general, 1918–19. Moscow, Lenin Library.*

НА КОНЯ, ПРОЛЕТАРИЙ!

№ 52

Рабочая революция должна создать

могущественную красную конницу.

Коммунист должен стать кавалеристом.

Л. Троцкий.

fied, and text became secondary to a violent image. It is interesting to note the similarities between the propaganda of the Bolsheviks and that of their adversaries. The former emphasized the principles of justice, revolution, and the defense of the poor against the return of the privileged; the latter affirmed middle-class fear and the desire of its members to preserve the status quo. But both sides, at least in their posters, created myths. The bleeding knife of counterrevolutionary propaganda was answered by the flaming sword of the Red army giant, as well as by the heroic worker, and—larger than life—Lenin.

The first Bolsheviks—who had known prerevolutionary times, whose intellectual background had taught them to debate ideas, and who were convinced of the importance of an exchange of views and of criticism—must have resisted this type of propaganda. Russia was a land of illiterate peasants, and the second generation of Bolsheviks was composed of militant and uneducated young people, representatives of a new working class with a rural background. Disciplined and kept in hand by the new secretary general, Joseph Stalin, they were more vulnerable to the simplifications already perceptible during Lenin's time. It was to them that posters asking for heroic efforts were addressed.

Hungarian Communist poster designed to combat pessimism and defeatism. Budapest, Szikra Kiadás.

153

Detail from a 1920 Red army recruiting poster by D. S. Moore entitled You Have Not Yet Volunteered? Moscow, Lenin Library.

To be able to hope for a future of joy and plenty compensated to a certain extent for extremely difficult conditions brought about by severe postwar famines and the resistance of Russian peasant farmers to collectivization. Poverty, the disintegration of the social order, and hunger characterized the years in Russia from 1919 to 1922. The Bolsheviks had to cope with acts of cannibalism in the Ukraine, gangs of abandoned children looting and robbing on the roads, the physical exhaustion of millions, and the destruction of property and harvests.

Meanwhile the Bolsheviks were hoping that the revolution would spread rapidly and inexorably over Western Europe and that Western workers would support the socialist effort. Bolshevik leaders were convinced that Germany, Italy, and then France would become Communist. And indeed there were serious social upheavals; Hungary, Germany, and even Italy were tottering.

A major reason for these upheavals was that the economic crisis that followed the war made radical solutions attractive to the masses. Soldiers returning after four years at the front could not find work; the wounded

and invalids could not survive on the moderate pensions that inflation-ridden governments could afford to pay them. Realistic posters with somber and often pathetic images reveal how hard life was for many. They show starving Russians, hungry children, an invalid former soldier gazing at his now useless tools, a downcast jobless man followed by his wife and child.

That poverty was admitted in these posters indicates a change in social attitudes. Nineteenth-century society had also been afflicted by poverty and unemployment, but the great mass of people who were affected had had few means of expression. In fact, the poor had been so influenced by middle-class values that they considered themselves responsible for the shame of their poverty or joblessness.

After the Russian Revolution the attitude of the poor and the unemployed began to change. They began to publicize the misery of their condition, and they held society, not themselves, responsible. They refused to be submissive; they refused charity; rather, they demanded satisfaction. In the face of their demands for justice the supremacy of

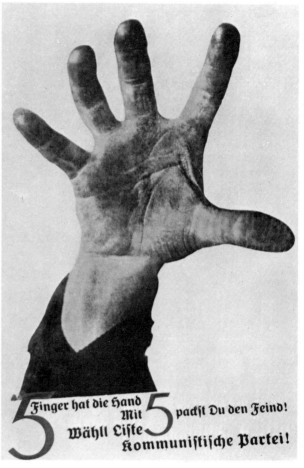

the middle class slowly began to give way.

This change could have been predicted. As the working class grew, its social awareness inevitably developed. Furthermore, publicity had spread the idea that new products were available to everyone. This awareness changed the expectations of the poor, who no longer accepted as fair the spending habits and the affluence of the middle class in the face of their own joblessness and hunger. The working class came to feel that revolts and demands for change were among their rights.

Why did these conditions not bring about the revolution the Bolsheviks anticipated? Why, on the contrary, did fascism win the upper hand in Italy in 1922 and in Germany ten years later?

To answer those questions one must remember the formidable upheaval caused by the war, not only in socialist but in right-wing thinking. The war experience had led many to rediscover the qualities of strength, discipline, and commitment to a nationalist ideology. Furthermore, the war had schooled members of the middle classes to assume authority. As officers they learned to command. But when they became civilians once again, they were unable to find work, let alone to lead. At the same time their self-esteem was further threatened by revolutionary movements that were questioning the war from which they had returned victorious. The war also produced large numbers of rootless men who drifted from place to place, unstable and adventurous; who had nothing to lose and everything to gain

Anonymous German poster of 1925 soliciting votes for the far-left-wing Spartacists, who opposed the Weimar Republic. Amsterdam, International Instituut voor Sociale Geschiendenis.

from joining an extremist group that offered power and prestige.

Governments felt threatened by revolutionary pressure. Industry, crippled by the postwar economic crisis, wanted to regain an upper hand and recover the losses it had sustained when salaries were raised to attract manpower during the war. These conservative political and economic tendencies laid the groundwork for fascism.

The nationalism that united the disillusioned middle class, veterans, and adventurers was an emotional, passionate nationalism tinged with mysticism. Fascism emerged as a kind of nationalism with religious overtones. In Rome fascism was lyrical; in Berlin and Nuremberg it was Wagnerian.

Fascism fascinated people with its manipulation of mob emotions, its mythological references, its emphasis on mystery and sacrifice. Fascism created new myths: that the state was all-powerful, that the party was in command, that race dominated, that force was the final arbiter.

In Germany in particular, economic chaos and a tradition of ardent nationalism made fertile ground for extremists. For several years Communists and Nazis struggled for political control. But whereas the Communists drew support from only one group, the working class, Adolf Hitler's Nazis appealed to a bitter middle class, to veterans who were unable to find work, and to malcontents from all levels of society.

Germany never really recovered from World War I. Instead it became the soil in which the seeds of the next war were sown. **157**

1925–1945
Propaganda
and Ideology

It was as though people were dancing the Charleston on a volcano—such was the mood of those crisis-filled years between the European tragedy that had begun in 1914 and the next great war.

People danced because they did not want to see what was happening. For the survivors of the war, physical exhaustion was proof that they were alive. If possible, they wanted to forget the economic crisis that spread from country to country in 1929; they wanted to forget the Nazi troops roaring "Sieg Heil" at stadium rallies; they wanted to forget that Spain was in flames, battered by a bitter civil war that pitted Fascists against Communists.

Each country, and particularly those that, like France, had been drained by the First World War, wanted peace at all costs. No cause was worth dying for—not saving Ethiopia, which the Italians invaded in 1936; not saving the Sudetenland, which Germany annexed in 1938.

Yet war approached, an even more terrible war than the one before, a war that would rage throughout the world. Once more those caught in the torment would look back with nostalgia on these few years between the wars—scarcely twenty years, not even the span of a single generation. For by 1939 the men who had fought in 1914, in the war they thought would make men renounce war forever, found themselves once more in uniform, sometimes side by side with their sons.

Dancing was one of the most popular forms of entertainment in the years between the wars. In Europe foreign rhythms were in vogue. The tango and the fox trot had been fashionable before the First World War, but now they became the craze. The Charleston arrived, and with it the fashion for music—and dance steps—derived from American Negro folklore. This was the beginning of the decisive influence that the American way of life would exercise on European civilization. The American army disembarking in Europe in 1917 had suddenly revealed a new world to the Euro-

158

Opposite: detail from a German poster by Walter Schnackenberg for the Odeon Casino nightclub, about 1925. Munich, Stadtmuseum.

peans. These lithe, beardless young men, with their cars and their khaki uniforms, their apparently relaxed disciplines, were the ambassadors of everything modern, from jazz to haircuts. They argued for an end to rules, for a liberation of the body, for straightforward behavior. From then on the average European considered America the ideal.

Everyone imitated the Americans. Dancing couples moved less stiffly: their knees touched, they held each other around the waist, their bodies pressed together. The dancers' audacious behavior indicated how much old standards were changing. The First World War accelerated this natural evolution, not only because Americans set the example but also because after every war or other violent social upheaval people become intent upon enjoying themselves.

The 1920's were characterized by a taste for the new. Black dancers and singers, who had been the rage in New York between 1910 and 1914, crossed the Atlantic after the war, and London, Paris, and Berlin applauded their syncopated rhythms. The blues became the vogue. In 1924 in the United States Paul Whiteman gave his first concert of classic jazz. European musicians soon discovered this new form; one of them, Darius Milhaud, made two trips to America to study it before composing his African ballet *The Creation of the World*.

European culture was soon pervaded by these new sources of inspiration, these new means of expression. United States influence grew even though politically it had entered a period of isolationism after the administration of President Woodrow Wilson. The triumph of black culture and folklore both in the United States and Europe suggests a change in attitude toward blacks. It was as if the war, having attested to the defects in European civilization and having undermined Europe's role as a moral and historical model, gave new vigor to dependent peoples. The acceptance by the "white" world of black art was an important step in the movement for black equality.

Jazz, blues, and Negro spirituals became broadly familiar to society at least partly as a result of the rapid growth of relatively new means of communication. Radios became commonplace at every level of society. In 1922 there were 60,000 radios in the United States; in 1928 there were 7,500,000. The radio imposed cultural and behavioral standards on great numbers of listeners without those listeners realizing what was happening. This subliminal influence was much stronger than that exercised by publicity posters, because the size of the audience was so much greater.

More and more noticeably, advertising was changing people's behavior by giving them standards to imitate. While it did not always invent them, often it made the standards of a small group familiar and desirable to large numbers of people. Influenced

by publicity, people, particularly women, continued to pay more attention to their appearance. In the posters of the time women were depicted as delicate, slender, refined. In the twenties the slim, elongated look became the dream of millions of women—but an unattainable dream for many because few can conform to a perfect model. The result of this kind of publicity was to make women constantly anxious about their appearance and therefore even more susceptible to the pressure of publicity. Publicists were quick to realize that women had to be convinced of the fundamental importance of their appearance before they would constantly restock their wardrobe, run to the hairdresser, or buy new cosmetics.

Publicity posters were the natural means of disseminating these new trends; and whether they advertised hats or flowers, they offered human models for imitation. Thus posters contributed to uniformity as much through the models they presented as through the mass sales they stimulated. Especially in cities, where posters covered sides of houses and buses, people conformed to norms established through advertising.

The same uniformity appeared in social behavior. As always, for instance, certain vacation spots were chic, and social pressure made trips to these places fashionable. In certain sets one *had* to go to seaside resorts, one *had* to know Deauville or the

Detail from a poster by Marcello Dudovich for the famous Italian hatmaker Borsalino, about 1930. Printed by Ricordi, Milan. Treviso, Museo Civico Luigi Bailo, Salce Collection.

Riviera, Menton or the Lido in Venice. More people wanted to own a radio, and if they could afford it, an automobile. But with these new products the motive of buyers was not so much to conform as simply to enjoy the new technological marvels. Standardization and mass production brought prices down. At the same time manufacturing became concentrated in giant firms which were so large that they no longer had to worry about competition. In France in 1929, for example, three firms produced 75 per cent of all the cars in that country. Fiat, Ford, Citroën, Renault, and Mercedes became household words.

The number of cars on the roads was growing rapidly. In 1911 there were 700,000 in the United States; in 1921, 11 million; in 1928, 24 million; and in 1937, 30 million. In 1930 France had 2,200,000 cars, compared to 110,000 in 1913; the United Kingdom had 2,400,000, and Germany 1,500,000.

The automobile was changing Western civilization technically, socially, and psychologically. Cars clogged city streets, and new roads were created for them. Highways bisecting rural landscapes were built in Germany and Italy. Urban areas, particularly in the United States, grew in circumference as people became able to commute by car from jobs in the center of the city to homes in the suburbs. Rubber plantations spread in Southeast Asia as the demand for tires grew; between 1913 and 1926 the index of rubber production in Asia jumped from 100 to 1,186. The rapidly growing automobile industry fostered numerous related businesses, such as gas stations and auto repair

163

shops. From the 1930's onward the automobile created a new way of life and helped set new standards.

Cars introduced mobility and speed into everyday life. Radio and the telephone accentuated this evolution toward rapid communication, an evolution that continued to bring people and countries closer together. The trend was furthered also by developments in aviation. The military significance of the airplane had become apparent as the First World War progressed; as a result governments had supported aviation research and development. At the end of the war large numbers of now-useless military aircraft came into the hands of civilians, many of whom became barnstorming stunt pilots who took part in air shows across the United States and Western Europe.

As more civilians became familiar with airplanes, the attitude that they were primarily military weapons changed, and the civilian aviation industry began developing. After 1925 private companies in the United States began carrying mail on airplanes. Charles Lindbergh first crossed the Atlantic by plane in 1927; the inaugural flight from Paris to New York was made in 1930. By the 1930's airlines were carrying passengers commercially, for profit. However, the number of passengers was limited; and although the volume of air freight tripled between 1932 and 1937, it was not yet sufficient to make the airplane a major factor in economic life.

Meanwhile, although a few military leaders—General William Mitchell of the United States, Italian General Giulio Douhet, Royal Air Force Chief Marshal Sir Hugh Montague Trenchard—argued that aircraft would play increasingly significant roles in future wars, few governments paid much attention to their pleas for the development of independent air forces. Among those countries that did take the development of air power seriously were Germany, Italy, and Japan. Germany and Italy took the opportunity to test the effectiveness of their air forces in the Spanish Civil War; beginning in 1936 they sent men and equipment to support Francisco Franco's Nationalists. The damage suffered by such cities as Barcelona and Guernica (the destruction of the latter was immortalized in a famous mural by artist Pablo Picasso) was new proof of the destructive power of airplanes.

By 1939, after these experiments in Spain, Germany and Italy were ready for the Second World War. Fighter planes could attain a speed of 350 miles an hour; bombers had a range of 1,200 miles. The world was soon to find out how deadly aviation had become.

If most people did not realize the horrors that would result when the most advanced technology was put at the service of barbarism, at least some were aware of a cli-

mate of tension and suppressed violence. This climate was frequently reflected in the arts, particularly in films. Many films powerfully expressed an uneasiness as well as a foreboding about the future of civilization.

One such film, the powerful *Cabinet of Dr. Caligari,* which opened in Berlin in February, 1920, is a philosophical fable that evokes the violence, crime, and destruction from which postwar Germany had just emerged. Its sleepwalking protagonist is compelled by his all-powerful master, Dr. Caligari, to become a murderer. In this sense the film recalls the war that had just ended and the millions of soldiers who had been forced to kill and destroy by those who lusted for power. *Caligari* also suggests that society resembles an insane asylum: the narrator, it turns out, is a patient in an asylum; the Caligari of his fantasy is the asylum's director. A mad world ruled by a dictator, in which people resemble sleepwalkers, had succeeded the disorder left by World War I. In that sense *Caligari* anticipated the coming of Adolf Hitler.

Fritz Lang's 1927 film *Metropolis* is another violent and fantastical evocation of the diseases of contemporary postwar

165

Detail from an anonymous 1935 poster advertising the trimotor Savoia Marchetti SM75. Printed by I.G.A.P., Rome and Milan. Treviso, Museo Civico Luigi Bailo, Salce Collection.

civilization, in this case the economic unrest seething in Germany. Lang's fable presents a conflict between the masters, living in paradisiacal splendor amid hanging gardens, and the workers, robotlike, laboring underground, servants of the machines. The workers rebel; but after a violent conflict in which the factory is destroyed, the tycoon and the factory foreman—Capital and Labor—shake hands in a gesture of friendship. *Metropolis* so impressed Hitler and his propaganda minister, Joseph Goebbels, that Goebbels eventually asked Lang to make Nazi films.

Films continued to grow both in popularity and lavishness. Fritz Lang's *Metropolis,* for example, took a year to make and required 620,000 yards of film; a cast that included 8 stars, 250 children, 25 negroes, 4,100 women, 1,100 bald people, and 25,000 men; and props that included 3,500 specially made pairs of shoes and 50 automobiles.

These immense expenditures—greater than were required in any other art—naturally forced film makers to take into consideration the number of paying spectators their films would attract. Consequently, writers and directors frequently tried to create works that would appeal to and express the feelings of the largest number of people. Possibly, therefore, films are the most accurate reflection of popular mood of a given time. Certainly in films public taste and the aesthetic and intellectual preoccupations of film makers meet.

If nothing else, the cinema gave the viewer an opportunity to lose himself in a romantic or heroic story, as well as to identify with the star. And he did not forget the movie as soon as it was over: back out on the street, the spectator might for a while become Rudolph Valentino or Gary Cooper, Greta Garbo or Marlene Dietrich. He might ape their dress or mannerisms, or simply feel different.

The power of the cinema was so great that it was held responsible for extraordinary things. In 1940, after the military and politi-

Detail from a poster for Queen Christina, *a famous Greta Garbo film. Treviso, Museo Civico Luigi Bailo, Salce Collection.*

Detail from a poster by Marcello Dudovich for the film Hold Your Man, *with Jean Harlow and Clark Gable. Printed by I.G.A.P., Rome and Milan. Treviso, Museo Civico Luigi Bailo, Salce Collection.*

cal collapse of France, a number of spokesmen for the Vichy government declared, along with the critic Georges Sadoul, "If we have lost the war, it is because of the film *Le Quai des Brumes*." Indeed, through the tragic fate of the deserter played by Jean Gabin, this film, which appeared in 1938, expressed the anxiety of the masses who felt ineluctably pushed toward war. That the spectators saw their fears acted out on the screen is one explanation for the tremendous success of the film.

Their fears were legitimate. Soon after Fascism had triumphed in Italy in 1922, the "brown plague" infected Germany. Gangs of storm troopers roamed the streets, breaking the windows of shops owned by Jews and spreading terror among the adversaries of Nazism. The considerable means available to Hitler allowed him to organize thousands of meetings, to print tens of thou-

Below: anonymous poster for the film Le Quai des Brumes, by Marcel Carné, with Michèle Morgan, Jean Gabin, and Michel Simon, 1938. Paris, Cinémathèque Française.

OVERLEAF: detail from an anonymous poster for Angel, a 1937 film by Ernst Lubitsch with Marlene Dietrich. Paris, Cinémathèque Française.

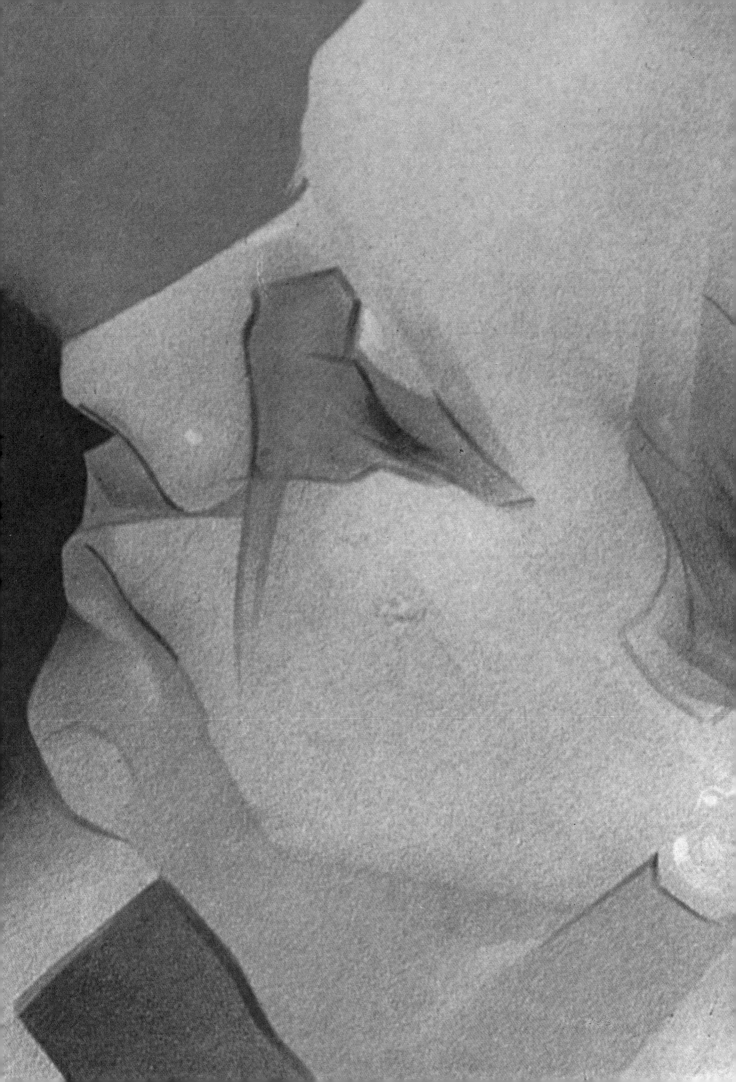

Poster by A. Dejneka. The caption reads: "We are sending workers to the Urals and the Kuznetsk Basin." These regions in Russia were being industrialized. Moscow, Lenin Library.

the capitalist countries considered the existence of the U.S.S.R. a greater danger. The U.S.S.R., in turn, felt surrounded and menaced by a coalition of capitalist nations. The propaganda campaigns waged by both sides encouraged simplifications. Particularly dangerous were those that led to the veneration of Joseph Stalin as the hope of Communism.

The struggle between pro-Communists and anti-Communists, as well as between various socialist factions, diverted attention from the Nazi menace. In Germany, for example, the opposing strategies of Communists and socialists kept them from uniting against the Nazis, which might have prevented Hitler from coming to power. Until about 1934 the working class itself was sharply divided, with some loyal to the Social Democrats and others to the Communists. Preventing any unity of action was

sands of posters, to pay his storm troopers. The financial resources of heavy industry were at the disposal of the man who promised to re-establish order in Germany, neutralize the Communist threat, and restore German pride and power.

Yet while Hitler was taking over Germany,

One of the first Nazi posters with the swastika, the sword, and the oak-leaf wreath, 1932–33. Stuttgart, Staatsgalerie.

Poster opposing anti-Semitic actions of the Nazis, entitled The Heroic Deeds of the "Pure Germans," *1934. Stuttgart, Staatsgalerie.*

Left and opposite: poster issued in French by the propaganda ministry of the Republicans in Spain protesting the bombing raids on Madrid by Franco's Insurgents, 1937. Paris, Musée des Arts Décoratifs.

the Communist assumption that the socialists and the leaders of non-Communist unions were all "social-fascists" or traitors.

One poster for the French Communist-led union, the Confédération Générale du Travail Unitaire, illustrates the level of oversimplification. A May Day demonstrator, stripped to the waist, powerful and symbolic, is about to be attacked not just by the police but by strikebreakers from an opposing union, the Confédération Générale du Travail, whose leader, Léon Jouhaux, is about to knife the striking worker. This poster reveals the obstacles in the way of cooperation among various liberal factions: their distrust of one another was almost greater than their distrust of their real foes.

Occasionally the Communists did cooperate with liberal and socialist parties in order to move governments toward more liberal positions. One example was the Popular Front government in France in the 1930's. But these popular fronts, quite apart from the internal difficulties inherent in all coalitions, had to face the direct aggression of their fascist and Nazi enemies.

This was certainly true for the Frente Popular in Spain at the time of the Spanish Civil War. Aligned against it were conservatives, the Catholic church, monarchists, the military, and the powerfully entrenched bureaucracy, along with their Fascist and Nazi allies. The contribution of the Catholic church was vastly important from the point of view of propaganda.

The posters issued by Franco's side presented the Insurgents' revolution as if it were a religious crusade. In one poster the

Anonymous French poster of the Communist-led Confédération Générale du Travail Unitaire, a labor union, for May Day, 1936. Paris, Bibliothèque Nationale.

Anonymous poster for Franco's Insurgents during the Spanish Civil War, 1937. Treviso, Museo Civico Luigi Bailo, Salce Collection.

174

shadow of a cross falls on Spain, suggesting that under the Nationalists Spain would teach the truth and guide the world, and would above all fight the "Reds," the incarnation of atheism, revolt, and absolute evil. These themes mobilized all those who were attached to tradition; they attempted to unite reactionary political views and the aims of the Catholic church. In reply the republican opposition pictured children crushed by the bombs of the Nazis and the Fascists.

One has only to glance at these posters to realize to what extent passions had overtaken precise analysis. The German Social Democratic party tried to counteract Nazi propaganda by showing a woman on her knees lacing a Nazi's boots, but the attempt probably did not achieve its goal. The appeal may have succeeded with some German women, but the majority were already too used to submission. And the image of the haughty, hard-eyed soldier armed with a whip and served by a woman might well have provoked a kind of fascination in male viewers, rather than strong condemnation. Ironically, although Russian posters stressed women's emancipation, the Soviet leaders

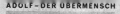

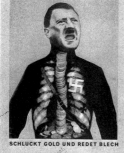

ADOLF – DER ÜBERMENSCH

SCHLUCKT GOLD UND REDET BLECH

YEARS OF DUST

RESETTLEMENT ADMINISTRATION
Rescues Victims
Restores Land to Proper Use

Far left: poster by John Heartfield in which Hitler becomes "the superman, eating gold and talking tin," 1932. Private collection.

Near left and below: poster by Ben Shahn for Roosevelt's agricultural programs, 1937. New York, Museum of Modern Art; gift of the artist.

were also building a repressive, dictatorial society.

In truth, neither socialists nor Communists understood the nature of fascism and Nazism. At first they saw the basis of these philosophies only as a classic form of reactionary ideology; later they thought of it as a political offshoot of the capitalist system. They did not grasp that it was an inhuman and regressive response to the most profound questions facing man in the twentieth century. One could not fight fascism and Nazism with arguments that appealed only to reason, because those ideologies relied not on reason but on people's unconscious fears and motives.

The battle with fascism was complicated by the economic and social problems that were tearing capitalist society apart. Nazism benefitted from the chaos caused by the economic crisis of 1929, which ruined millions of people and caused long lines of unemployed to form in front of soup kitchens. No country, whether fascist, communist, or democratic, escaped the effects of the Great Depression, which brought poverty to American farmers as well as to workers in the industrialized Ruhr section of Germany.

In the United States, where capitalism was not threatened by an extreme left wing, the system survived, thanks to Franklin D. Roosevelt and the New Deal. But in Germany, where compromise was precluded by the strength of the Communists and their practice of fragmenting the opposition, the choice was between Nazism and revolution. When faced with these alternatives, the established political, economic, and social authorities united against revolution. Hitler became the beneficiary of their decision.

The public, which always puts its own security first, hesitated for a long time before finally opting for the fascists and the Nazis. Eventually carefully organized and controlled elections rallied hesitant voters to the Duce and the Führer. But these elections came after Fascism and Nazism had already triumphed, after they had gained

178

power through political manipulation and strong-arm tactics. Public opinion thus rallied around the party that had already won, and around one man—Duce or Führer—who became the incarnation of fatherland and government.

Myths grew up around Mussolini and Hitler as they did around Stalin. These men were regarded as father figures, geniuses, warriors, even artists. Mussolini, who was the most theatrically inclined of the three, was variously shown flying a plane, reaping a harvest, swimming like a champion, or giving a history lesson to the Italian Academy.

Crowds were organized to acclaim these men, whose pictures appeared in increasing numbers on walls. At their personal appearances, lighting, colors, and sounds were all coordinated; once the stage was set, the leader would materialize dramatically to the roar of his fanatical supporters. On posters showing these leaders, words had all but disappeared. At most the posters bore a few words—"Heil Hitler" or "Si" when they were inviting people to vote yes in a plebiscite. Otherwise, the image was enough.

The new regimes tried to establish a religious or feudal relationship between subject and master. This is why ceremonial rituals using banners, uniforms, and emblems were invented. The public Hitler and Mussolini always wore the military trappings of their office, the insignia of the new order that they were establishing. Until early in the 1930's, Mussolini often appeared in civilian clothes, like the chiefs of foreign states he was meeting. But after the Ethiopian war and the triumph of German Nazism, he appeared only in uniform. Posters after 1935 show him helmeted, with his jaws clamped shut and his face set in what he believed to be a heroic expression.

When Hitler and Mussolini met, they met both as leaders of government and as the commanders of their armies. Although they were civilian heads of government, their dress was military.

Fascist principles enjoyed relatively strong support despite—or perhaps because of—their archaic nature. However, when one evaluates the popularity of Nazism and to a lesser degree of fascism, one must take into account the importance of police pressure and people's fear.

Hitler and Mussolini established hierarchic relations among people and organized them into groups according to their ethnic background and their race—a throwback to the most regressive periods in history. They presented themselves as conquerors; they glorified violence, the importance of weapons, and the nobility of death.

Anonymous British poster of 1941. London, Imperial War Museum.

At the same time the Nazis successfully borrowed themes from the far left (they called themselves National *Socialists*, for instance), emptying them of their real content and keeping only the forms. One poster, showing an arm in chains on a red background, suggested that when the crowds raised their arms to approve the Führer's actions, when they shouted "Ja," with that word they broke the chains that bound them. It was as if Hitler's victory was the victory of the revolution. Unmistakably, the poster was capitalizing on widespread socialist sympathies.

Fascist propaganda particularly influenced the thinking of the young. Both Nazism and fascism were presented as youthful ideologies fighting the old order. They glorified virility and health. The mass sporting events and the discipline they offered satisfied the needs of a large number of young people, as did the songs, uniforms, competitions, and affirmations of nationalism. The young were carried along, seduced by parades and posters like the one showing a joyful, athletic member of the Hitler Youth running against the background of a flag with a swastika.

With the Italian invasion of Ethiopia in 1935 and the beginning of the Spanish Civil War in 1936, the contagion of war reached southern Europe and northern Africa. In the next decade war engulfed the world, leaving countries in ruin and tens of millions dead in Europe alone, from the banks of the Volga to the Channel beaches, from the Nile to the Apennines. And there were more dead on the other side of the globe, on Pacific islands and on the bare hills of China.

For the civilian populations the war was terrifying, because they as well as the soldiers were under fire. Each side tried to bring down its enemy through terror, to break down its economy, and to raze its cities. Barcelona, Guernica, Warsaw, and Rotterdam were bombed. Paris capitulated and chose to live for a while on its knees. But England withstood the Luftwaffe's onslaught, even though London was bombarded and Coventry was destroyed.

The belligerents no longer tried to conceal what a few years earlier would have been considered unwarranted aggression against unarmed civilian populations. In fact propaganda made use of it: posters proclaiming that London was destroyed showed houses in ruins and heavy smoke enveloping its ancient monuments. War had become total, and there was no longer a distinction between civilians and combatants. Those who ordered the raids made the spectacle of a city in flames a lesson for everyone: posters proclaimed that one side was capable of wreaking such destruction on the enemy, and that the enemy would retaliate in kind if given the chance. Total war truly involved the whole population.

By rejecting the distinction between civilians and soldiers, the war encouraged the involvement of the civilian population in the battle. This was especially true of the Germans who fought behind their Führer's banners until the end, for they were well indoctrinated, faithful to their military traditions of courage and persistence, and convinced that if Hitler was defeated Germany would be punished. In 1945 the people of a battered Germany rose in a body to stop the headlong advance of the Red army, which to them was the supreme threat, possibly because Germany feared what Russian troops would do in retaliation for the pitiless and barbarous war Hitler's troops had waged in the Soviet Union.

After the initial German onslaught, civilians in occupied countries slowly began to resist. Nationalistic feelings revived even where they had been stifled. Moreover, it was most often the masses who fought to restore national independence after the elite had capitulated.

While some countries were quickly overrun, in others the invaders met with more stubborn resistance. When Italian troops invaded Greece in 1940 they encountered stiff popular opposition. Greek women carried cases of ammunition to the front over difficult mountain tracks. Everywhere par-

Britain's new Airborne Army goes into action in Europe.

BACK THEM UP!

tisans rose against the occupiers, and Greece successfully rebuffed the Italian invasion. The next year, however, the country fell to Germany.

Contrary to the situation during the First World War, there was no similarity between the adversaries. World War II was a confrontation between two opposite conceptions of life and politics, not the clash of equivalent imperialisms. The battle was between victims and their oppressors, between freedom and dictatorship, between civilization and barbarism.

For this reason there could be only one front. Of course there was a line along which the regular armies fought each other in the conventional way, but behind this front in enemy-held territory there were areas occupied by partisans. Sabotage be-

181

ΟΙ ΗΡΩΙΔΕΣ ΤΟΥ 1940

came a common tactic. Airborne troops parachuted into enemy territory in defiance of traditional strategy.

New legends grew up, not around the pilot or the submarine captain, as they had in the First World War, but around the partisan and the parachutist. In the First World War the hero was the man who was master of a machine. During World War II, when armored divisions were composed of thousands of tanks and when squadrons of planes crisscrossed the skies of Europe every night, the operation of machinery seemed a pedestrian task. The new heroes were the men who fought without machinery, like the partisan fighting a guerrilla-type war or the parachutist dropped behind

enemy lines armed only with light weapons.

This is not to say that machinery was not decisive. Despite popular exaltation over the exploits of commandos and partisan units, everyone knew that industrial power and technological know-how would tip the balance in the end.

The mobilization of material in addition to human resources was considered to be of the first importance. In the occupied countries the Germans rounded up all salable merchandise and raw materials, leaving local populations to manage as best they could. Only by buying black-market goods could civilians supplement their insufficient rations. The poverty **183**

Opposite: anonymous Greek postwar poster entitled The Heroines of 1940, *celebrating the women of the resistance. Brussels, Musée Royal de l'Armée et d'Histoire Militaire.*

BACK THEM UP!

Left and below: anonymous British poster of 1942–43. Milan, Museo del Risorgimento.

brought about by enemy plundering was an important factor in the awakening of national feelings and the will to resist.

To replace the many goods no longer available, such as coffee, tobacco, sugar, textiles, and leather, ersatz versions appeared. Everything possible was salvaged: statues were melted down, copper and glass became extremely valuable, meat bones were exchanged for laundry and hand soap. A way of life very different from the plentiful prewar times became the norm, as millions learned to adapt and make do.

The situation was not the same in all the Allied nations. In the Anglo-Saxon countries rationing was limited or nonexistent; but Russians suffered great hardships, and their living conditions were made more difficult by the harsh climate. Everywhere, however, in Russia as in England and the United States, people concentrated on conserving energy and increasing production. In Russia factories sprang up beyond the Urals, with women replacing men as workers. In fact women participated in the struggle even more than they had during the First World

Below: anonymous British poster intended to cement cooperation between Russian combatants and English workers, 1944. Milan, Museo del Risorgimento.

Bottom left: anonymous British poster picturing and quoting Winston Churchill, 1940. London, Imperial War Museum.

Bottom right: anonymous British poster of 1940 emphasizing the unity of the Commonwealth. London, Imperial War Museum.

War, serving in the army, fighting with the partisans, working in factories or intelligence operations. The line separating the activities of men and women grew blurred.

In this new type of warfare, steel, gasoline, and the production capacity of factories were decisive assets. Therefore, as soon as Europeans saw the United States enter the war, they were convinced that Germany would lose. For Europe looked on the United States as a country of vast resources, which finally would enable the Allies to defeat the Axis powers.

When the American and English armies landed in Normandy at dawn on June 6, 1944, their success was primarily a result of their superior equipment, which gave them undisputed command of the skies and the sea. Also, the Allied army, unlike the Germans, was able to pour fresh troops into battle.

By 1944 the German army was no longer the invincible force it had been in the spring of 1940. It was exhausted in particular from its efforts in Russia, where it had been confronted not simply with the Russian army but with the resistance of a whole population, as well as the terrible climate. A turn-

185

Soviet poster by V. A. Serov entitled Let Us Defend Mother Volga, *1942. Moscow, Lenin Library.*

Small British poster by Abram Games, which was put up in barracks and other interiors, 1943. Milan, Museo del Risorgimento.

Small Italian poster by Boccasile entitled The Enemy Is Listening, *1941. Treviso, Museo Civico Luigi Bailo, Salce Collection.*

ing point in the war had been the battle for Stalingrad, on the Volga River. Late in 1942 the German army had taken that city, house by house, in fierce fighting marked by heroic efforts on both sides. But Russian troops counterattacked, the Germans were unable to hold out, and in February, 1943, General Friedrich Paulus surrendered. Stalingrad was in ruins, and tens of thousands were dead. But Russia, by proving that it could hold its own in the face of a massive German effort, had scored an immense psychological as well as military victory.

Westerners did not hesitate to praise the bravery of the Russians. Winston Churchill, who was one of the fiercest enemies of the Communists between the wars, collaborated with Stalin. The man in the street considered "Uncle Joe" in the Kremlin a

respectable and valiant ally. During the Battle of Stalingrad the eyes of the world were focused on the Russians defending the Volga; many sensed that the capitulation of Paulus' armies at Stalingrad was the beginning of the end for the Third Reich.

The public support given the U.S.S.R. and Western recognition of the Kremlin as an ally had strong ideological repercussions. In fact these occurrences marked the end of twenty years of anti-Soviet feeling. The consequences of this about-face were the more pronounced because by the Second World War whole populations were aware of and responded to military and political decisions. The alliances between countries were no longer simply agreements worked out by diplomats; public opinion had a bearing on the effectiveness of such al-

liances. But public opinion in turn could be influenced, especially by effective propaganda.

The Second World War was a war of rival propagandas. For example, the British beamed broadcasts to the occupied countries to bolster the morale of the population, direct the combatants, and instruct the many intelligence agents working in enemy territory.

Radio London and Radio Moscow were used as weapons. Propaganda was no longer a peripheral but a major force in the conflict: it was used by the Allies to win the support of people in Axis-occupied territories and to persuade them to fight back, to spy, and to threaten the Germans from all sides.

This kind of warfare constituted the great-est possible danger for all civilians: because one could not tell who the partisans were, everyone was assumed to be guilty; therefore anyone could be held responsible for the deeds of someone else. Again and again civilian hostages paid with their lives for the deeds of partisans.

At the beginning of the war German propaganda made every effort to convince the people in the occupied countries of the Germans' desire to protect them. This was especially true in France, which enjoyed particular consideration because of its strategic importance and its policy of collaboration. German propagandists had to make collaboration seem reasonable, to make it appear to be the first step in building a new Europe that the German army would protect from British and American rapacity and Bolshevik savagery. In propa-

Below and right: German propaganda poster by Boccasile used in Italy. The caption reads: "Germany is really your friend." Treviso, Museo Civico Luigi Bailo, Salce Collection.

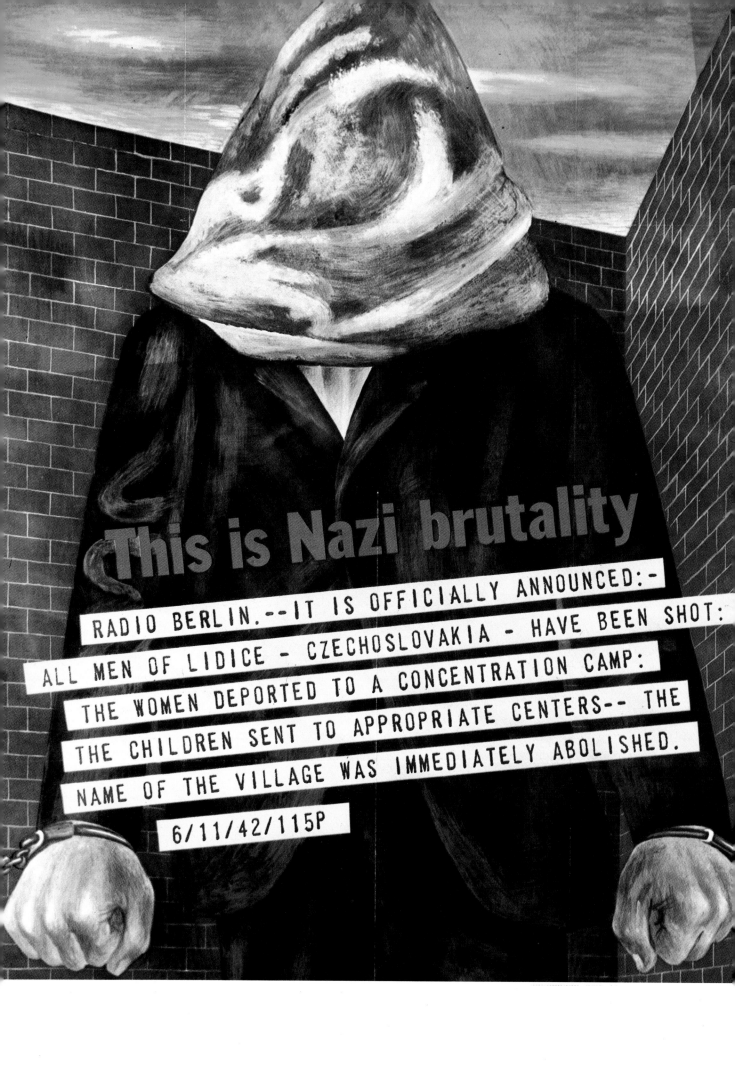

ganda posters German soldiers look vigorous and gay; they are shown holding out a brotherly hand or giving food to children.

Germany also had to attract millions of workers to replace Germans enrolled in the armies of the Reich. In the beginning German propaganda in France, for example, tried to organize a "relief" composed of prisoners of war and voluntary workers. When these attempts were not sufficiently successful, the Germans instituted the Compulsory Work Service. But the plan backfired somewhat because it aided the recruitment of partisans: those who refused to go to Germany became fugitives forced to hide in the country or in the mountains, where eventually they joined partisan groups.

By its very nature German propaganda

could not be successful. Collaboration could never be a relationship among equals, and the peoples Germany conquered could never accept an inferior role. Yet Hitler's propagandists, trapped by the logic of their racist theories and their affirmations of Aryan superiority, could only repeat that one must have "confidence in the German soldier," and that "great Germany will protect you."

German propaganda reflected the attitude of a colonizer addressing populations lacking culture and suffering from economic underdevelopment. Such an attitude was entirely unrealistic: the Dutch, French, or Poles of the 1940's were not like the nineteenth-century populations of Dahomey or Cameroon. Their countries had long, rich 191

Right and opposite: one of the first posters from liberated Paris. The caption reads: "The snipers and the partisans have spilled their blood for the people of Paris." Published by the Forces Françaises de l'Intérieur, 1944. Paris, Bibliothèque Nationale.

Below: proclamation by General Charles de Gaulle from his headquarters in London exhorting all Frenchmen to continue fighting, 1940. Paris, private collection.

expressed on the poster denouncing the "Jew behind the enemy powers" were only an excuse for genocide. Jews were first forced to wear the yellow star and were excluded from public places; next they were isolated in ghettos, and finally they were destroyed by the millions in such concentration camps as Auschwitz or Treblinka. All this was possible partly because the Jews themselves did not recognize the danger until it was too late, but mainly because the world was apathetic.

But people in other countries also knew Nazi brutality. They knew that the Nazis were quick to punish; after Reinhard Heydrich, deputy chief of the Gestapo, was killed in Prague in 1942, German soldiers executed the entire male population of Lidice, Czechoslovakia, and razed the village. They did the same in Italy at Marzabotto, in France at Oradour-sur-Glane, and countless times in Eastern Europe and the U.S.S.R. The Gestapo and the S.S. became symbols of evil, a nightmare come true for millions of people.

Everyone was frightened. Later in the war fear was replaced by revolt, but in the beginning the tendency was to retreat and to refuse to act. For the Nazis, meanwhile, repression on a large scale was a logical offshoot of their racist ideology. For them the world was divided into masters and their inferiors; the latter could be eliminated without discussion if it served the needs and interests of the former.

Until 1942 only small resistance groups, impelled by patriotism or ideology, were engaged in the fight against Germany. Most often they simply gathered information; but soon they began performing acts of sabotage and—often at the initiation of the Communists—carrying out assassinations. Eventually the ranks of the resistance were swelled by those outlawed for refusing to join the compulsory work force.

From 1944 onward the resistance mobilized hundreds of thousands of people all over Europe who were ready to help the moment the Allied armies disembarked in

histories, often with strong traditions of independence.

One appeal German propagandists could and did make in their posters was to anti-Semitism and racism, which had been relatively dormant in Europe for centuries. Jews were presented as the inspiration behind the anti-Nazi coalition. An apelike black American soldier was shown carrying off the Venus de Milo. In these posters Nazi propagandists tried to suggest that the Reich was the protector of all European civilization.

No matter how it was presented, German propaganda documented the brutal character of Nazism.

No other race was treated as inhumanly by the Nazis as the Jews. Ideas such as those

Normandy. Yugoslavia, Italy, Greece, and France had veritable armies of partisans led by such prestigious commanders as Charles de Gaulle and Tito. Their struggles quickly became legendary, sparking even greater efforts and enthusiasm. In France, for instance, the heroic efforts of the resistance contributed heavily to the successful Allied efforts to drive out the Germans after the landing in Normandy in 1944.

In August, 1945, the United States dropped the first atomic bomb on Hiroshima. The bomb did more than end the war in the Pacific; it introduced a new weapon of previously unheard-of destructive potential. For the first time humanity had at hand the means to destroy itself.

The bomb established for a while the military superiority of the United States, and it opened an age in which two superpowers would dominate the world. From 1945 on, despite public clamor for international disarmament and despite a growing peace movement, nations raced to join the atom club, while the United States and Russia struggled to establish political spheres of influence and military supremacy.

In 1919, at the end of the First World War, people thought that they had seen the last war. In 1945 the mushroom cloud over Hiroshima and Nagasaki reminded everyone how destructive man had become. The atom bomb was a watershed in human history. It ushered in a new era, the atomic age in which we live.

1950–1970
Words and Images

The year 1945 saw the end of the death and destruction brought by the Second World War; but it also marked the onset of a new kind of war—the Cold War.

With the collapse of Nazi Germany, the tenuous alliance between Russia and the Western allies came to an abrupt end. It was replaced by a bitter struggle between the two power blocs in which the antagonists, while avoiding general warfare, fought each other with every other available means: guerrilla warfare, propaganda, spying and sabotage, economic and scientific rivalry, a struggle for either influence in or control of neutral territories.

At the end of the war Joseph Stalin wasted no time extending Russian influence throughout Eastern Europe. By 1948 most of the countries of Eastern Europe had become Russian satellites, with puppet governments and economic plans that put Russian needs first. The United States in turn, after Russia's expansionist intentions became apparent, committed itself to a policy of containing the Soviet bloc. In a major effort to counteract Russian aggression and help those countries still free of Communist domination to rebuild, the United States instituted the Marshall Plan, which poured massive amounts of economic aid into Europe. It also abandoned its traditional avoidance of peacetime alliances and in 1949, with eleven other nations, signed the North Atlantic Treaty, a defensive military alliance. Once again, this time through NATO, Western Europe was armed, with a standing army ready to counter Russian threats.

Russia responded to the presence of NATO troops by establishing its own defensive alliance, the Warsaw Pact. Despite this maneuver, its Western expansion was effectively contained. Its efforts in Western Europe thwarted, Russia turned its attention to Southeast Asia, encouraging Communist guerrillas and rebel governments in Malaya, the Philippines, Indonesia, and China. In China the Communists achieved their most spectacular success: by 1949 they were in control of the entire country.

But it was in Korea that the Cold War became hot, when the United Nations in 1950 authorized its members to send troops to aid South Korea, which had been invaded by Communist North Korea. Both United States and Communist Chinese soldiers fought in Korea, and the threat of a nuclear confrontation loomed.

In fact what made the years after 1950 particularly terrifying was the very real threat of nuclear war. The United States monopoly of nuclear weapons had ended in 1949, when Russia exploded its first atomic bomb. Then, in response to Korea, the United States began a major rearmament effort. Russia meanwhile was rushing to build a nuclear stockpile, and several other nations were working to develop their own atomic bombs. International tensions were so great that nuclear holocaust sometimes seemed unavoidable and even imminent.

While governments were pursuing policies that could conceivably result in the destruction of civilization as we know it—even in the decimation of the human race—many individuals and groups were urging disarmament, in the interests not simply of world peace but of world survival. In their efforts to win supporters, these organizations waged intensive publicity campaigns to educate the public about the threat and the effects of nuclear war. One shocking poster by Hans Erni said it all: an atomic war could destroy the world.

Following the end of the Second World War, Western European countries were faced with the staggering task of revitalizing their ruined economies. They succeeded spectacularly, largely because they abandoned some of their traditional nationalist rivalries in favor of European economic integration. The first step in this direction was the Marshall Plan. The United States between 1948 and 1952 authorized $17 billion to help Europe recover from the war; these funds were allocated by the participating countries themselves, through the newly formed Organization of European Economic Cooperation. This united effort

Opposite: poster by Hans Erni protesting atomic war, published in several languages by the Swiss movement for peace, 1954. The Italian caption reads: "Let us stop it." Printed by Atar, Geneva. Zurich, Kunstgewerbemuseum.

IMPEDIAMOLO

MOUVEMENT *SUISSE* DE LA PAIX · SCHWEIZERISCHE BEWEGUNG FÜR DEN FRIEDEN · MOVIMENTO *SVIZZERO* PER LA PACE

AFFICHES ATAR, GENÈVE

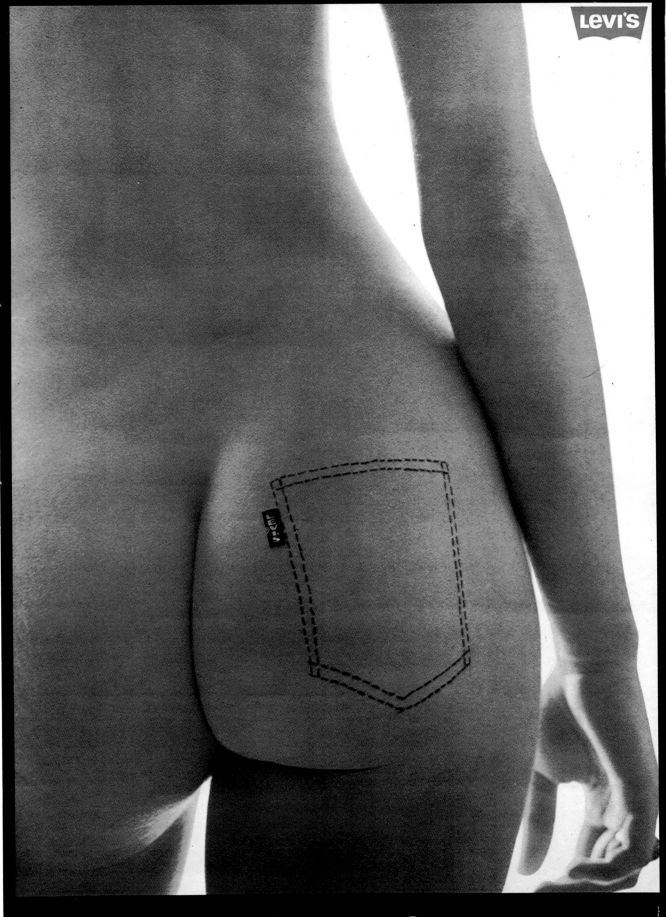

was followed in turn by plans for actual integration through a new organization, the Common Market. Politically, too, NATO had paved the way for closer cooperation.

Meanwhile, as Europe moved away from intense nationalism and toward unity, nationalism flared in other parts of the world—especially Africa. There the colonial powers loosened their grip, and country after country became independent.

The postwar economic boom in Western Europe led to a significant change in the life style of the average European. More than ever, industrial countries became consumer oriented. Advertising posters offered goods to buy, places to go, entertainment to enjoy. But no longer were middle-class Europeans the only group being urged to buy automobiles, television sets, clothes, airplane trips. As consumers were urged to spend, these goods became available to the working class, thus further eroding what once had been a significant distinction between classes.

Advertising posters had also been changed in an effort to make them appeal to the broadest possible audiences. After the war posters became simplified and stylized. Increasingly, products were allowed to speak for themselves, and many posters had

little or no text: the shape of a Citroën was enough to indicate its make; the word "Levi's" was sufficient to identify a widely known product. Also, especially in United States posters, the impact of photography was apparent. Thus a poster advertising Miss Levi's uses a naked woman, but it is no longer the frozen, marblelike figure common in earlier posters; rather, this advertisement is marked by photographic realism. And an ad for Swissair uses an actual photograph of jet engines.

Ironically, the products and opportunities that liberated so many imposed new constraints at the same time. The proliferation of the automobile, for instance, raised many new problems, particularly in crowded urban areas. Among these problems were traffic jams, pollution, and a growing accident rate.

Roads formed arabesques through the countryside for speeding cars. Roads and cars pervaded everyday life. For many urban people their car was a means of escape to the country, and it was thus seen as an instrument of freedom and power. Such were the myths that helped sell cars. Whatever the reasons, car sales boomed. And because automobile manufacturers consequently became such an important sector **199**

SWISSAIR

of the economy, in the United States especially government economic policies favored the automobile and related industries at the expense of urban public transportation.

The myth of the car as a means of escape to a purer place does not take into account murderous traffic jams like the one that Jean-Luc Godard showed in exemplary and prophetic fashion in his film *Weekend*. In urban areas especially, newspapers, radio, and television report on road conditions and traffic jams. On weekends mass departures from the city take on the aspects of general mobilizations. The driver seeking solitude and wide-open spaces is trapped in an immobile column of thousands of vehicles like his own. The crowd is no longer a group but a series—a lonely crowd, as American sociologist David Riesman calls it. The people in it are not really free; they are trapped by the very machine they consider an instrument of freedom.

One hazard of automobile transportation is that as cars increase in number, so do accidents. Some of the causes are mechanical, others human. Potentially dangerous is the frustrated driver trying futilely to make progress along a crowded highway. He may try to regain a semblance of initiative by driving faster, by passing a long line of immobilized cars. The result may well be an accident.

In many countries public and private organizations wage publicity campaigns to educate drivers about their obligation to drive cautiously. Posters such as the one in which a terrified child runs from the wheels of a car are enlisted to help reduce the number of accidents. Appeals are made to good sense and prudence, and speed limits are imposed.

During the 1960's there was a growing awareness of new constrictions imposed by the widespread availability of goods. These constrictions were felt particularly among members of the younger generation, who did not share their parents' veneration of objects. In the advanced countries automobiles and television sets became commonplace, and both their liberating and alienating qualities are now recognized. However, the younger generation, having found that it could not change the habits of society as a whole, simply refused many of the products of an industrial consumer society.

Meanwhile, breaking with a long economic tradition that favored continual expansion, some economic theorists questioned the wisdom of encouraging unlimited economic growth. They held that countries should desist from setting ever greater economic goals and instead set themselves limits that they would pledge not to exceed.

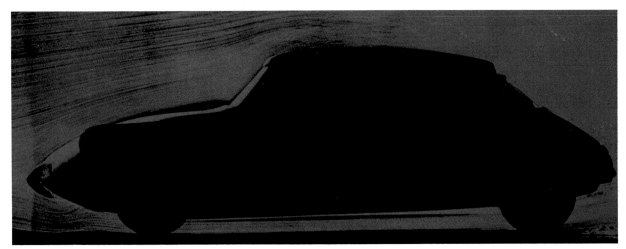

Poster by Theobald inspired by the film Easy Rider, *1970. New York, Personality Posters.*

According to this analysis, beyond a certain point the cost of industrial growth outweighs its benefits and produces serious social disruptions.

This fear that the world would change by the pressure of production and consumption is much more understandable when one considers the appearance of new evidence, day after day, of the side effects of uncontrolled growth. The inevitable consequence of industrial development is a modification of nature, which often means damage to the environment.

Damming a river can change the ecology of a whole region: it can affect plant and animal life; it can affect agriculture; it can bring about the end of leisure and survival activities such as fishing. Spills from tankers carrying oil to satisfy the endless demand for fuel in industrial countries can destroy ocean life. Tankers that flush their tanks near the coast can create a "black tide," which ruins beaches, kills birds, and destroys marine life. A sad contradiction of our times is that as more and more people have time and money for vacations, many of the places they might go are ruined by pollution. Moreover, the beaches are becoming as crowded as cities.

All elements are being transformed: the air is polluted by oxygen-devouring supersonic planes; the water is polluted with sewage; and the ground is saturated with chemical wastes. Man can only be terrified by this thorough and rapid corrosion of his environment, which is depriving him of the surroundings he has known for thousands of years.

Man is suddenly beginning to fear processed foods, chemical products, polluted water. Ironically, these fears have led to new and flourishing industries, which offer such products as bottled water, health foods, and chemical substitutes. The search for the "natural" in the products one buys and in the life one leads is affecting more and more levels of society. People in many parts of the world are expressing the desire and the need for a life without artifice.

Throughout the 1960's students in particular rebelled—against war, the establishment, industrial society, and in general a way of life and an attitude that put goods and profits before people and their environment. Student revolts—over issues that ranged from petty grievances to major ideological differences—rocked universities across the United States and Europe. At the root of the uprisings was a profound dissatisfaction with contemporary values and with the effect that the pursuit of these values was having on the world.

Many of those who rebelled in the so-called privileged nations were also objecting to the enormity of the gap between the haves and the have-nots, between the developed and underdeveloped countries of the world. In light of the profound poverty in which so many lived, these young rebels

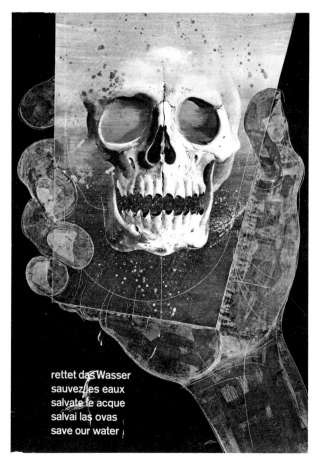

rettet das Wasser
sauvez les eaux
salvate le acque
salvai las ovas
save our water

HELP THE R.S.P.C.A. TO STOP OIL POLLUTION

Below: 1962 poster by Abram Games, published in several languages by the Food and Agriculture Organization of the United Nations in their campaign against hunger in underdeveloped countries. The Spanish caption reads: "War on hunger."

Bottom: poster by Josef Müller-Brockmann (graphics) and Ernst Albert Heiniger (photograph) entitled Protect the Children, 1958. Published by the Swiss Automobile Club. Zurich, Kunstgewerbe-museum.

found what they considered excessive consumption to be particularly distressing.

Advertising reflected this growing unrest through an increase in the number of posters supporting various political and social causes and expressing ardently felt convictions. Posters campaigned against atomic weapons, pollution, hunger, overpopulation, and especially in the United States, the Vietnam War.

Yet while these problems were seen as worldwide, crossing national boundaries, the absence of propaganda on the need for the world to unite in a common assault on its problems is striking. Effective planning on a worldwide scale is the only solution, because the problems affect everyone. Yet there is a notable lack of information about worldwide solutions, and few posters treat social evils. One has only to compare the thousands of posters offering typewriters, television sets, and beer to the few depicting the poverty on other continents to measure people's ignorance of the real state of the world. Perhaps posters reminding us that the number of illiterates in the world had increased by 100 million in less than 25 years, or that in the year 2000 there will be a world population of 6 billion people, of which 4 billion will be undernourished, would help us understand the problems of our time.

For the West, perhaps the most divisive struggle of the 1960's took place not in Europe but in the Far East, in Vietnam. As United States involvement deepened, and as the casualty rate—of both Vietnamese and United States soldiers—rose horrifyingly, protests against the war mounted.

Throughout the decade the United States continued to pour men and equipment into Vietnam. Yet United States firepower, its new methods of warfare, its bombs that showered steel splinters, its napalm, and its defoliants, which were intended to make the jungle disappear—all of these did not make a South Vietnamese victory possible. The war dragged on year after year.

Never before had a war been so intensely

"No thanks, Eve. I'd rather have an apple."

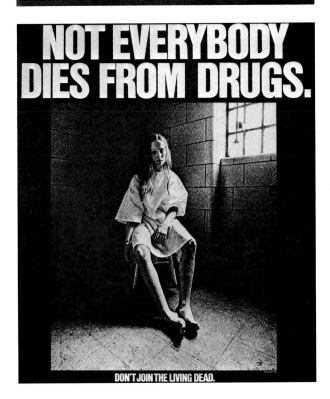

NOT EVERYBODY DIES FROM DRUGS.

DON'T JOIN THE LIVING DEAD.

covered by the news media. Reporters and photographers had fleetingly captured the horrors of other wars in the twentieth century; but in the sixties, for the first time, television brought daily, lengthy evidence of what the war was like and what it was doing to Vietnam. This steady barrage of film, much of which suggested that the Vietnamese people themselves were but pawns, fueled the antiwar protests, which grew in intensity.

In the United States many members of the younger generation, especially students who were subject to military service, revolted. Some fled to Canada; some sought loopholes to avoid the draft. Others, young and old, staged demonstrations, marches, prayer vigils, sit-ins; pacifists even broke into draft offices and burned records. Outside the United States Vietnam became for some a symbol of United States aggressiveness. Western Europe had its share of antiwar protests. In both Europe and the United States striking posters were used to arouse public opinion against the war. One in particular summed up the change in attitude toward war that had taken place since 1945. It used the famous World War II photograph of United States soldiers raising the American flag on Iwo Jima; here, however, instead of a flag—symbolic of military conquest—the soldiers raise a flower, a pacifist symbol.

Of course United States involvement in Vietnam also had many supporters. Some believed the United States had an obligation to fight Communism wherever it threatened. Others, especially soldiers and former soldiers, could not bear to think that they had suffered in the name of a mistaken effort and that so many had died for nothing.

As the war continued both sides became increasingly bitter and even violent. Vietnam divided the United States as almost no other issue had in recent years.

In Europe, at least young radicals considered it possible that the East might come to dominate the West. They no longer drew their instruction in revolution from Euro- **207**

End Bad Breath.

pean history, but from events in such faraway countries as Cuba and China. When news of revolutions in those countries reached Paris and Rome, the events took on a romantic, heroic aura. The details were unimportant. Thinking that they were applying "concrete analysis to a concrete situation," young people dreamed of using in Europe methods that had worked under the guidance of Fidel Castro or Mao Tse-tung.

At the time of their revolutions, of course, neither China nor Cuba was yet part of industrial civilization. This fact too was appealing to young revolutionaries. Their unwillingness to accept the negative consequences of progress and their fear of a society that destroys its natural environment contributed to their enthusiasm for what happened in Cuba and China.

Among the heroes of young radicals were Castro and above all the late Che Guevara. Posters of Che rivaled in popularity those of popular singers. The young identified with the resolute, passionate hero with the faraway expression, the man who gave his life for a cause. After his death, long hair like Che's became popular; books, movies, and plays about his life appeared.

Ironically, through his appearance on posters and as the subject of various entertainments, this revolutionary hero of the anticapitalist left made money for exactly those capitalist entrepreneurs his followers professed to despise. In contemporary Western society, everything is potentially a source of profit.

Below: antiwar poster by Ronald and Karen Bowen, using Rosenthal's famous Iwo Jima photograph of 1945 in a photomontage, 1969.

Opposite: detail of an antismoking poster by Peter Max entitled Life Is So Beautiful. *New York, American Cancer Society.*

In fact, to capitalize on dissent has become a modern trend. The hippies' protest of the sixties, an extreme antiestablishment movement, became the theme of musicals, and the hippie style of dress became fashionable. Publicity posters glamorized the new, freer attitudes of young people in order to sell one or another drink or to celebrate the virtues of a shampoo or a car. One French publicity poster showed employees standing on their desks looking out of windows. The caption read: "Don't be afraid to stand on X metal office furniture to see the demonstration." And on another French poster a squad of women as though on the march shout, "We want X shampoo!" These shifts indicate to what extent the consumer society is flexible; there seems to be no form of behavior that it cannot eventually accept and even market.

These posters suggest the ultimate frustration—at least in the West—of those who have attempted to find a different way of life or who have protested the old one; they also suggest the impossibility of escaping from the relentless dictates of a consumer society. Modern Western culture seems able either to digest everything or to relegate everything that is really corrosive and indestructible to the safe fringes of society. Politically, there have developed in Western industrial countries opposition parties that really do represent an opposition, or incumbent administrations that take into account a variety of attitudes in the existing society. One result is that many protesters, acting according to what is perhaps a law of history, either compromise or capitulate.

Those who question the existing order face not only social pressure from within each country but international pressure as well.

The two superpowers, the United States and the Soviet Union, each possessing the power to destroy the planet, still are tremendously influential in international relations. Certainly there are notable differences between the two countries. In the United States young people can question the system and make their opposition known. In a country where publicity is part of daily life, even politics is a publicity fair: presidential candidates have to be sold to voters in posters and television spots, and both major political parties buy radio and television time and rent billboards, like any company wanting to advertise and sell its products. In the Soviet Union, on the other hand, everything is done very quietly: politics is low-key, secretive, often repressive. Dissenters daring to express their feelings are a closely watched, often persecuted minority. Control over politics is more efficient in Moscow than in Washington.

Nevertheless, many feel that the two powers are no longer at opposite poles, perhaps because no longer does either incarnate an ideal. In some ways they are moving closer together: as the Soviet Union becomes more consumer oriented, social

welfare programs receive more attention in the United States. Whereas at one time ideological differences stood in the way of any economic relations, now practical considerations overshadow ideological ones. Russia welcomes United States private investment, while the United States welcomes the opening of new markets.

The change in Russian-United States relations began in 1953, after the death of Joseph Stalin. Of course there was no sudden or steady improvement. Both sides were intermittently aggressive: the 1961 Cuban Missile Crisis, for one, brought the world perilously close once again to a major confrontation. A new area of competition opened when Russia launched *Sputnik I,* the world's first artificial satellite, in 1957, and when the United States sent up its first satellite, *Explorer I,* in 1958. From then on the space race intensified. Meanwhile espionage continued as a major international activity that occasionally—as in the case of United States spy pilot Francis Gary Powers —became public, bringing damaging publicity to one side or the other and setting further barriers in the way of reducing tensions.

Nevertheless, gradually tensions were lessened. The heads of government became, if not warm, at least civil in their relations. After a massive arms build-up on both sides, both seemed to recognize an urgent need to control the arms race. While the road to disarmament remained long and tortuous, at least discussions were under way when both sides sent serious negotiators to discuss a Strategic Arms Limitation Treaty (SALT).

There were also changes taking place within Russia, as more emphasis was placed on producing consumer goods and the standard of living rose. Russia had also begun to turn its attention to the Middle East as a likely part of the world to establish its influence. Finally, and perhaps most important, Russia and China were drawing farther apart, and their borders were becoming increasingly tense as hostility led to frequent exchanges of gunfire. Pressured by

China in the East, Russia found that its best interests lay in improving relations with the West.

Inevitably, once political tensions lessened and the arms race was reduced, talk of trade between the two countries began. The result was that by the early 1970's, for the first time since the Second World War, Russia and the United States were officially doing business together. And as contact between the countries increased, culturally and socially their citizens seemed less strange—and less threatening—to one another.

By the mid-1970's the cultural and social separation was greatest between the West and the Far East, not between the United States and Russia. To many, especially revolutionaries, the future lay in the East.

The West's dream of the Orient has two sides. One is physical escape to the East, where one can submerge oneself in drugs or in contemplative philosophies. From time to time there appear in Paris or in American cities groups of young people, their heads shaved, wearing saffron-colored robes. Chanting rhythmically, they file through the streets to spread the teachings of the Orient. After decades of Western exploitation in Asia, including the opening of China by force, this seems a curious reversal.

In fact, Far Eastern philosophies and religions have become fashionable. Even among the vast majority who do not actually travel to the Far East, meditation and disciplines such as yoga have become increasingly popular. Even Eastern fashions are influencing Western styles. After President Nixon went to Peking in 1972 Chinese themes became popular in advertising. Soon posters appeared inviting people to buy "Mao fashions," and Mao-style jackets became the season's clothing fad.

The West's dream of the East has another side to it as well. For some the revolution to be accomplished by following the thoughts of Mao Tse-tung is attractive. In Western and Eastern Europe a small but

DEBUT

D'UNE LUTTE

PROLONGEE

ardent band of Maoists can be found, particularly in universities, urging revolution and criticizing both Western governments and other socialist ideologies.

At least in part, the appeal of Maoism and other extremist ideologies lies in their idealism and the total commitment they demand. Russia and the West no longer demand this fervent dedication to a cause; their economic successes have rather led to a loosening of the demands made on individuals. But for many, rigid discipline and a

revolution that promises no less than total social upheaval are appealing. These young revolutionaries are not yet caught up in the consumer mentality. Prolonged schooling has encouraged the freedom from materialism that they feel.

Of course only a relatively small minority have actually refused to accept or have denounced the system. But this minority has had a measure of sympathy from many young people, as was clear in May, 1968, in Paris, and earlier on the campuses of both American and Eastern European universities. It seems in fact as if a growing portion of the young have managed to escape integration at least for a while.

The emergence of China as a major world power has been one of the most significant developments in recent years. In the period immediately after 1949 China was intensely suspicious of and hostile to the West, especially the United States. China also became a major antagonist of Russia, accusing that Eurasian giant of selling out the Revolution. While China feuded with Russia, threatened the West, and concentrated on building a nuclear arsenal, it also encouraged and supported Communist revolutions in Southeast Asia and vied to establish its influence in Africa and the Middle East.

The result of all this international activity was the emergence of a new power bloc, known as the Third World bloc, comprised of small nations that had aligned themselves with neither Russia nor the United States. China, with its military development, became the leader of this new bloc. As the balance of international power shifted away from Europe and the West, Russia and the United States found their dominance in world politics being eroded as China's influence grew.

In the light of China's growing prestige and power, the United States finally relinquished its long-standing policy of ignoring China. Backing away from unremitting hostility, President Richard M. Nixon in 1972 undertook a historic diplomatic mission to

Chinese poster celebrating the joys of family life and work. Photographed in China by Van Moppès.

Humorous American poster parodying a series of advertisements for a woman's cigarette, 1972.

China. His visit was followed by slow but unmistakable signs of thaw: the beginnings of trade, of travel, of diplomatic relations.

Europe meanwhile continued its efforts toward integration, working out Common Market stumbling blocks that had for a time kept Great Britain out. As a unity Western Europe found itself doing quite well economically, holding its own with the United States, Russia, and Japan, which since 1945 had undergone a period of stunning economic growth that made it one of the world's leading trading nations. As these nations prospered, and as they also adjusted to shifts in the political balance of power, their citizens tried to make sense out of conflicting trends that tore them between accumulation of goods and antimaterialism, consumption and conservation, permissiveness and authoritarianism, liberalism and conservatism.

To a greater or lesser extent changes in attitudes and styles, as well as political trends, have been reflected in posters. In this sense the poster can accurately be called a mirror of the times.

1970–1990
Fragmentation of society, uniformity of the image

As the 1960's drew to a close the fissures in the fabric of society were still visible. May 1968 was a very recent memory. The philosophy of allowing market forces free rein and the demands this made had yet to stifle everything that turbulent time had symbolized. The determination of those who refused to conform had not yet weakened. The so-called consumer society had yet to hold unchallenged sway; in the highly developed Western democracies young people dreamed of imitating the revolutionaries of the Third World; they believed in the possibility of building an alternative society and it was this hope, this Utopian dream which had provided the inspiration for the movements of May 1968 all over the world. A mere twenty years sufficed for all these aspirations to be engulfed by the oncoming tide of realism.

Deep-seated historical trends were at work, transforming basic conditions; toward the end of the 1960's nowhere in the world was left untouched by the resulting upheaval, the outward manifestation of these revolutionary changes. The center of the economic activity and prosperity shifted westward, to the Pacific ocean which, with California and Japan on its eastern and western shores, became the center of the new global economy. The entire production process was being transformed: the age of electronics, computers, robots, microchips, and miniaturization and, before long, of biotechnology, had arrived to replace the labor-intensive industries inherited from the nineteenth century.

These major changes in the workplace and in technology shattered the long established order of society. In the "older" industrialized countries (Europe, the United States) the unemployed could be counted in tens of millions but at the same time new jobs in the service industries were being created. As a result, new lifestyles have been adopted. The day of the vast working class masses is done, the army of the proletariat has ceased to exist. Although urbanization continues all over the world, the millions of people who live in close proximity with each other now lead isolated, albeit similar, lives, detached from their fellow men as they stare at their computer screens.

In such conditions the media inevitably play a central role; a highly profitable industry has developed which links these countless separate individuals and provides them with a similar environment, spoon feeding them with a "media soup" in which the ingredients are soap operas, advertisements (commercial breaks, posters or other printed publicity material) trailers, film clips, and news programs. All these elements are used to make up the cultural bath in which we are all submerged.

During the last twenty years our planet has been besieged by images; we have been invaded by another reality, in which the goods we produce, our consciousness and our behavior are almost direct reflections of society's conformist values.

As a result, only fringe minorities still cherish dreams of building society along alternative lines; there are now only a few residual pockets of resistance to question the way in which capitalist societies and economies function. The twenty years from 1970 to 1990 will go down in history as those which saw the triumph of the market economy (or, more accurately, the practical application of a capitalist economy) in all societies. We have only to look at what has happened in European societies: values are those of the "winners," those who earn money, for money is king; critical attitudes are stifled. Even in China and the U.S.S.R., the second of these two decades has witnessed the encroachment of market forces as a result of the failure of their socialist, centralized economies.

By the time these two decades had run their course the world had changed completely. One has only to think back to the beginning of the 1970's and remember how American imperialism and more specifically its military expression was condemned all over the world.

Each country had its "Anti Vietnam War" movement, with campaigners who demon-

Opposite: poster by Alain Le Quernec for Amnesty International (detail).

**Arrêt de l'agression américaine
Paix au Vietnam**

Parti communiste français

strated in support of the Vietcong, glorifying the Communist fighters and portraying them in terms of mythic images. American imperialism was identified with high density bombing, with the use of napalm; it was perceived as synonymous with aggression, and capitalism implicitly indicted, seen as the enemy of socialism which in turn was equated with the Vietnam freedom fighters.

Against this background, the election of Allende as Chile's new President of the Republic was seen as a further setback for imperialism, progress for the anti-capitalist revolutionary forces. Conversely, the legitimate election of the Chilean president, who supported reform rather than revolution, was read as a danger signal in Washington: no sooner had Allende been elected than steps were taken to put an end to this prog-

ressive experiment. Allende's fall in 1973, when Pinochet launched his military takeover, signaled the triumph of the forces of reaction. And the solidarity shown with "the Chilean Struggle" was echoed by the fight against American imperialism.

These were to be the last blows dealt to the Western powers by the so-called anti-imperialist movement. The fall of Saigon, the American withdrawal (1975), the stabilization of the situation in Chile, and the departure of "Western" troops from African territories, meant the end of anti-colonialism and anti-imperialism. From then on the newly independent former colonies and the Latin American countries were left to face their own internal problems; sometimes caused by ethnic or tribal confrontation, sometimes by regional conflicts in which the great Western powers were only indirectly involved, avoiding direct incrimination.

POLITICAL PRISONER

LONG KESH

ONE OF MANY MEN ALMOST BEATEN TO DEATH BY BRITISH TROOPS
AFTER THE BURNING OF LONG KESH CONCENTRATION CAMPS ON THE
15th OCTOBER, 1974.

Issued by Belfast Sinn Fein

To be war not to be?

The seventies and eighties are therefore an era characterized by political change throughout the world. Irreconcilable economic interests set nation against nation, and the oil price hikes and embargoes deepened the crisis. In the United States the Watergate scandal led to President Nixon's impeachment and resignation; Britain had to cope with the Northern Irish question against a background of increasingly frequent sectarian killings.

But these scattered conflicts could not obscure the central question facing the world: disarmament or nuclear destruction? War or peace? This dilemma became ever more pressing with the proliferation of nuclear weapons and capability; in 1974 India became the sixth power to join the nuclear club.

Was it this menace, the threat to the survival of mankind, which led to the popularization of behavior which had traditionally been that of a privileged minority? A taste for pleasure, to the point of hedonism; a rejection of restraint; a desire to satisfy urges with little or no effort; a longing for a return to nature; the advent of the age of leisure. All these ideals, apparently bequeathed by the sixties, were articulated by the rioters and strikers of May 1968 and encapsulated in graffiti on the walls of Paris buildings. This new outlook on life became a mass phenomenon. Individualism was part of the baggage of those who set out on the quest for private happiness and from then on formed part of the creed of Western collectivities. Advertising — and posters were no exception — delineated and accelerated this trend. In the poster shown on page 221, the Place de la Concorde in Paris has been transformed into Central Park or Hyde Park, with people stretched out on the grass, talking amongst themselves, a setting perfect for day-dreaming. Clothes —

220

E' IN EDICOLA

Il quaderno del **SALE**

500 bastimenti carichi di...

a pagina 44 un nostro
servizio esclusivo dal Quirinale

Pino Zac, Italy, 1977. Cover of a satirical magazine, its theme the Lockheed scandal involving the then president of the Italian Republic, Giovanni Leone, and other well-known figures in France, Belgium, Japan, and elsewhere.

this advertisement is for Levi jeans — mold themselves to the body, revealing and emancipating it at one and the same time, free and flowing, no longer stiff and starchy. This new liberty of the clothed body expresses the individual's desire for enjoyment and sensual pleasure, and it underlines an unrestrained delight in the world and in other people, evidence of the contemporary evolution in morals and manners.

Nothing could be more inimical to this vision, to these attitudes than a hierarchical society (symbolized here by the geometrical, ordered architecture of the buildings in the Place de la Concorde against the skyline) and organized political life, with its parties, their ideologies for the organization of society and their collective aims. This poster reveals a widening gulf

Pacha Bensimon, France, 1974. Advertisement for Levi's. The non-conformist style of previous years is transformed into a more disenchanted view of the world that nevertheless retains elements of a radical change in fashion. Paris, Musée de la Publicité.

221

Below: anonymous, Palestine (occupied territory), 1988. Poster commemorating the twelfth anniversary of the founding of the Palestine Liberation Organization (PLO). The state of Israel, represented by the shattered Star of David, is still represented as the obstacle to be defeated. Paris, Musée d'Histoire Contemporaine.

between conflicting attitudes which were to become increasingly polarized: on the one hand life lived with personal satisfaction as its aim, and on the other a political world still imprisoned within the framework of the past.

Inevitably the parties and movements which stood for anti-capitalism, with their legacy of collective values and their hierarchical structure, were hardest hit by these changes. All over the world Communist parties were to find themselves in a state of crisis. Sooner or later, depending on the country, their support collapsed, undermined by the fact that the Soviet system had patently failed.

The most fundamental and pressing of the problems Western Communist parties had to face, not least because it was

Above: Israel, 1976. The condemnation of Zionism by a UN resolution dents Israel's image. Even a music festival becomes a means of restoring the image of an efficient, modern, harmonious country. Paris, Musée de la Publicité.

unthinkable to sever their links with the U.S.S.R. even when she no longer seemed a suitable "social model," was the fact that the communist analysis of society had now been called into question. Despite worldwide economic crisis and trade wars, Marxism itself seemed to be on trial, its ideology identified with the nineteenth century and condemned as totally inadequate when applied to twentieth-century society. A French Communist leader had declared in the 1930's: "Communism is the world's youth." Now its image was elderly and out of touch. Under the circumstances it is understandable that sporadic efforts were made to update this image, to appeal to the late twentieth century. The French Young Communist Movement's poster shows Karl Marx as a hitch-hiking hippie who is a wise old patriarch with a kindly smile, in a bid to put a convivial, modern 223

Paul Davis, USA, 1977. American Indians are one of the oppressed minorities drawn to the attention of public opinion.

Below: Bachs, 1979. In declaring 1979 the International Year of the Child, the UN sought to stress the often startling situation of the world's children, particularly in under-developed countries. Paris, Bibliothèque Forney.

face on traditional revolutionary symbolism. The poster typifies an attempt to adapt that stood little chance of success.

During this period of transition, political forces had been universally weakened. Respect for the workings of parliamentary democracy had been sapped by scandals unearthed by the press and given very wide currency by the media in general. All over the world oppressed minorities tried to make their voices heard: Basques, Kurds, North American Indians, Armenians, and many others. The reverberations of their struggles and of other localized conflicts, muffled or stifled to a greater or lesser extent, threatened cohesion and conformity with fragmentation and dissent. While sovereign states struggled to pursue an apparently logical course of standardiza-

año internacional del niño 1979

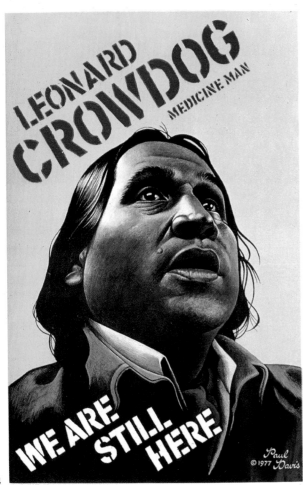

tion and unification, a *de facto* standardization already owed its existence to the images disseminated by the media, not least through television's vastly popular series and soap operas.

Amnesty International was founded with the purpose of trying to ensure that humanitarian principles were respected by those involved in these local, usually internal conflicts. Amnesty sought to harness and organize public opinion, using moral pressure to defend political prisoners.

Proclaiming 1979 the International Year of the Child, with this joyful poster to publicize it, was certainly a positive step, the sign of a new awareness, but children are still the main casualties in deprived areas. Hundreds of thousands of them are still dying every year, victims of malnutrition or

224

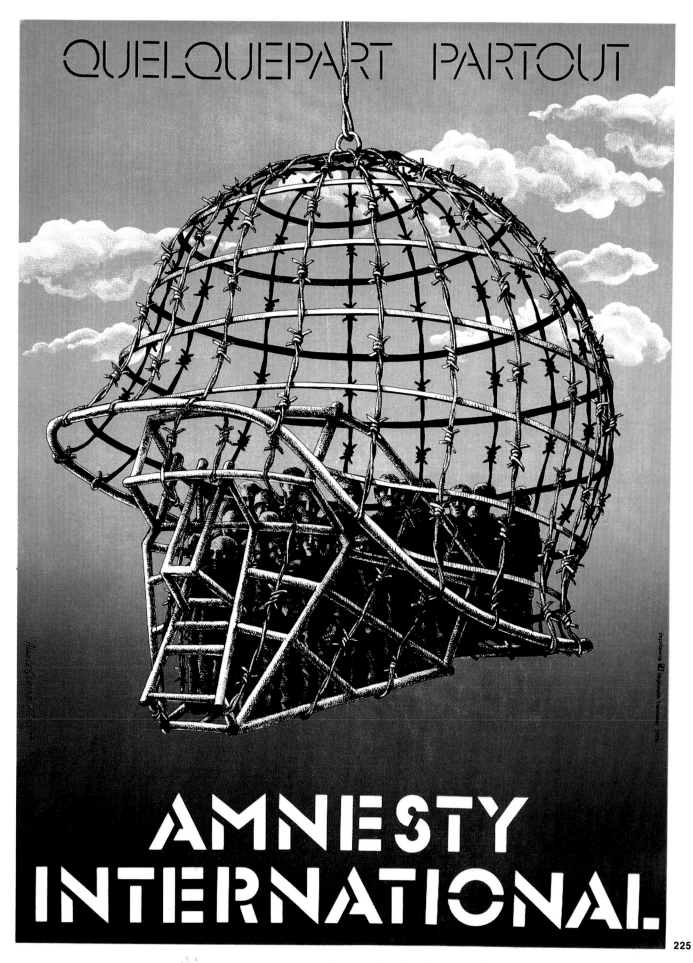

QUELQUEPART PARTOUT

AMNESTY INTERNATIONAL

Alan Le Quernec, France, 1978. Torture, summary executions and the violation of human rights surface throughout the world. Amnesty International sets itself the task of defending each single case. Paris, Bibliothèque Forney.

lack of medical care. Children are abused by their own parents or by other adults; they are sold, and exploited in all sorts of ways.

Only a worldwide commitment to change could alleviate such suffering. Compared with such cruel realities, politics as practiced in the developed countries resembles a superficial game, a luxury enjoyed by rich nations and affluent societies. In this context, the French Socialist party's poster describing Giscard d'Estaing's term of office as President (1974—1981) as "seven years of misery" certainly smacks of hyperbole when compared with the social problems confronting other countries, but each citizen can only measure conditons with the yardstick of his or her own individual, everyday experience. There is a widespread perception of reality as a broken mirror: electoral promises were, and are, shattered once a party actually assumes power,

CHOISISSONS LE PARTI SOCIALISTE

Above: Alain Le Quernec, France, 1980. The French presidential elections draw near and the image of efficiency and modernization of the president in charge, Giscard d'Estaing, is shattered. Paris, Bibliothèque Forney.

bringing only disillusion for those who voted them into office. .

Society is, moreover, increasingly preoccupied with non-political issues. Behavior and morals underwent a rapid change in the 1980's.

Despite widespread poverty, the only expression of rebellion has been the popularity of loud, pulsating rock music. Young people flocked to mass concerts and few other events could draw such vast crowds. Such collective activities (sometimes espousing worthy causes, such as the Band Aid appeal), have coexisted with a surge of individualism: each person in his or her own little world, alone with the Walkman.

New preoccupations began to make their presence felt. In the 1980's ecological movements were founded that stressed the danger to the planet from all things nuclear. New political parties demanded "an alternative energy policy" to protect the natural world. This met with a cool response in many countries until the late eighties, after the Chernobyl disaster in the Soviet Union.

During these years inhabitants of the developed countries have derived a vicarious satisfaction through supporting "heroic" political causes. This involvement at several removes has usually been inspired by altruistic and wide-ranging human rights questions. Condemnation of South Africa's policy of apartheid and racism has been widespread: the face of Nelson Mandela, leader of the ANC and the world's oldest political prisoner, became the symbol of a solidarity of principle always expressed in words rather than deeds.

All these factors have contributed to the present tendency to turn politics into morality, as if politicians, the actors on the political stage, will only capture their audience's attention if they avoid talking politics overtly. As a result politics has acquired an increasingly apolitical image. Politicians with a high media profile assume other personae: the keen sportsman or sportswoman; the family man; the reader or (better still) writer of novels, and so on. They have become media celebrities. The Smile counts for far more than The Message. The latter, such as it is, amounts to a few apparently spontaneous catch phrases which, far from being uttered on the spur of the moment, have been carefully thought out by the P.R. men.

While the language of obfuscation may

227

France, 1981. Advertising campaign by the ECOM-UNIVAS Agency to promote the use of the Paris underground railway. Paris, Musée de la Publicité.

POUR UNE AUTRE POLITIQUE ENERGETIQUE

PSV
BRETAGNE

Alain le Quernec, France, 1984. The Chernobyl disaster has yet to happen, but the accident at the Three Mile Island nuclear power station (28 March 1979) has aroused strong feelings against nuclear power on the part of left-wing politicians and nascent ecological organizations.

be neutral, anodyne, conformist or hermetic and predictable, the citizen's response takes the form of graffiti or finds an outlet in violence and escapism. Or it can be expressed by posters which challenge the consensus, like slaps in the face for all those who see them. If they are to attract attention they have to hit the passer-by smack between the eyes.

Slick, glossy posters that offend no sensibilities have had their day. Surprise is of the essence, even when considering political and other highly charged issues. Nowadays, political posters are illusive: the Italian Communist Party's poster (page 231) is not without its partisan element but this is no longer the primary message. An unexpected image on arresting phrase is used such as *Vietato vivere! (It is forbidden to live!)* Once this has grabbed the attention of the passer-by and he or she reads on, then — and only then — does it become clear that this is a poster promoting the Italian Communist Party, by which time it is too late

Christer Temptander, 1985. The repression in the black ghettos of Johannesburg and the awarding of the Nobel prize to Bishop Tutu draw attention to the fight against apartheid of which Nelson Mandela becomes the symbol. Paris, Musée d'Histoire Contemporaine.

to prevent the catch phrase from registering; it has already delivered its message.

The same approach was chosen to promote various left-wing and centrist political youth organizations which cite the latest Spanish Constitution as proof of their legitimacy. The strange figurehead catches the eye, inviting closer examination to work out what the poster is all about.

Drug abuse is a main issue, in our society. The very word "drug" conjures up images of degradation and violence, and some people feel more comfortable if they can avoid mentioning it. The impact of the poster on pages 232–233 comes from proclaiming in banner headlines: "Drug abuse: let's talk about it." Instead of provoking an automatic rejection, the aim is to attract, to enter into a dialog with a public drawn by the sight of two enchanting children radiating the calm contentment and innocence of 229

Grapus, Italy, 1984. Poster created by the Grapus group for a graphics exhibition held at Cattolica, Italy. Paris, Bibliothèque Forney.

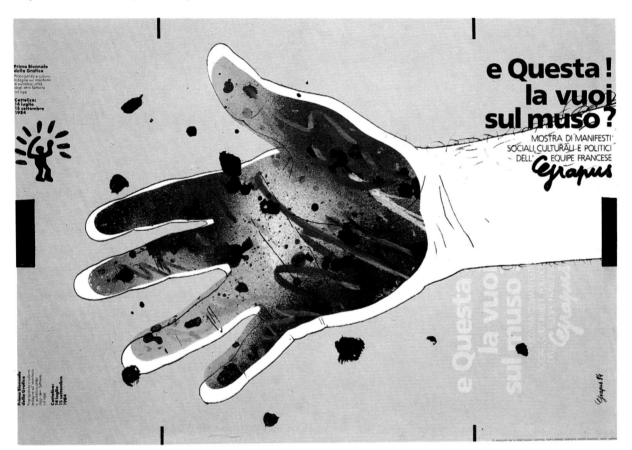

Grapus, Italy, 1984. Poster created by the Grapus group for a graphics exhibition held at Cattolica, Italy. Paris, Bibliothèque Forney.

youth. There is no need for the poster to supply the words "Save us from drugs": the sight of these potential victims is enough to trigger a train of thought, ending in a silent appeal deep in the mind of the onlooker.

From this, and from the previous posters, widely differing in style, it is obvious that direct promotion of a point of view is no longer effective: today's method is to suggest, to convince by stealth, disarming the prevailing mood of skepticism.

Even during an election campaign, when most stress should theoretically be placed on electoral programs, the posters which actually register with the voter are those that ignore this convention. The blasé and suspicious passer-by must be caught unawares, startled, intrigued, then won over.

In the run-up to the French legislative elections of March 1986 which were to decide the fate of the Socialist government,

the message was not "Support the Left! Vote Socialist!" Instead the posters illustrated in an exaggerated form of caricature what the return to power of a right-wing government would mean: "Help! Give us a hand! The Right is creeping back."

The political parties have no wish to challenge this preference for passive acceptance through refusal of any alternatives, as against reasoned conviction. They believe that they can only tinker with the situation, that they are so shackled that their freedom of action is very limited. It is best to make as few promises as possible, for they cannot be kept. In such a climate, they begin to despair of bringing about a much needed change. Even if this were possible, they fear the turmoil in its wake. But if politics surrenders this ground, we may well find ourselves at the mercy of other forces. Society could, for example,

find itself driven by its own fears disrupted by the extremism these emotions generate. During the two decades of 1970—1990 the threat of nuclear war has appeared to recede somewhat, especially once discussions on nuclear disarmament were under way; the presence of Gorbachev as leader of the Soviet Union seems to promise a breathing space in international relations, but meanwhile other dangers have loomed.

One of these is terrorism, often linked to a surge in militant Islamic fundamentalism (Iran being the obvious example). Even in a world apparently dominated by very advanced technology, with the developed countries rejecting politically inspired violence, attitudes inherited from the past still persist. They can even surface in industrialized societies when fear of a "plague" starts to spread among them. This has happened with AIDS. Long dormant, atavistic

impulses reawaken, showing how insubstantial the veneer of civilization really is.

Sadly, scapegoats have already been chosen to blame for this loss of freedom: those who are HIV positive, the carriers of the AIDS virus, anyone, by extension, whose way of life leads people to infer that they may be victims of the disease (such as homosexuals and drug addicts) and consequently a threat. In practice AIDS will be unstoppable if we cannot manage to appeal to each person's individual conscience. Somehow we have to instil sufficient fear of the disease into drug addicts to make them decide to kick the habit, or at least never to share a needle. Somehow people have to be persuaded of the necessity for safe sex. It is certainly not beyond medical research, with all the vast resources at its disposal, to discover a vaccine sooner or later, or at least a treatment to mitigate the **231**

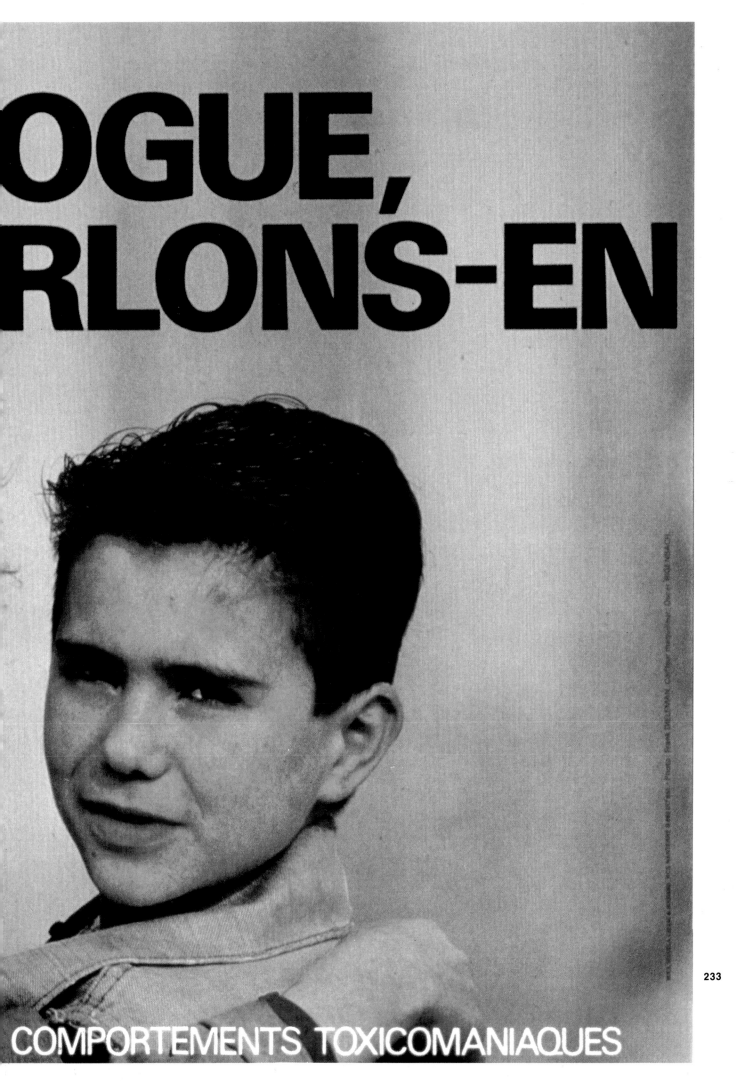

OGUE,
RLONS-EN

COMPORTEMENTS TOXICOMANIAQUES

ravages of AIDS.

The real dilemma, however, concerns the morals and values which provide a framework for the edifice of society. The individual is being asked to live his or her life — at least where drugs and sex are concerned — along prudent lines, yet is simultaneously urged to take advantage of immediate access to a limitless supply of sexual partners.

In some countries pornographic films are shown as early as 8.30 p.m. on some television channels which need no special access decoder. Scenes of murder, rape, and horrific violence predominate. Viewers exposed to these sights, especially the young, are having their sense of what is right and wrong molded in a spectacular and at the same time insidious way. Children are far more deeply affected by these

scenes and stories than by their schooling which has now been relegated to just one of the many ways they learn how society expects them to live.

Individualism, the impatient pursuit of maximum gain and pleasure are now the watchwords for behavior. Any effort to take account of the community's interests is limited to the absolute minimum: avoid breaking the law. In developed societies, however, laws are based on ill-defined ideological foundations, rarely on religious principles or "higher values." The only fear which remains is that of repression. Society is being torn apart. On the one hand, the laws of the market foster increasingly individualistic behavior and growing autonomy when it comes to taking personal decisions. These are channeled toward instant gratification. On the other hand, there must be

TBWA, Italy, 1987. AIDS has become one of society's gravest problems. This poster urges drug addicts not to share needles.

Beneix, France, 1987. Drive against AIDS by the French Ministry of Health. The poster is taken from a television advertisement. Paris, Musée de la Publicité.

235

controls to hold these forces in check, since society cannot function without a bare minimum of rules.

In order to make people observe these rules, now that appeals to individual "reason" (made through poster publicity, the spoken word etc.) often go unheeded, there is increasingly frequent recourse to threats and the use of fear and punishment. This has led to the proliferation of both state police and private security forces. In societies where values and moral principles no longer count for anything, protection and, if this fails, retribution, are the order of the day. Images can portray this situation more clearly than any number of sociological analyses. In contemporary films and television serials or soaps the action alternates between two locations. One is the family's little world, as restricted as any ghetto, isolated in the midst of society. All the action takes place in the same sort of surroundings: a house, an apartment. The various members of the family exit and enter. Then the location switches to the street (the outside world) where men and women are targets for violence, isolated individuals out in the city jungle.

In these same crowded city streets, full of people and cars, the façades of buildings are plastered with posters extolling pleasure and encouraging passers-by to indulge in all sorts of excessive consumerism, both material and sexual. The world of fantasy is constantly being stimulated, contrasted with the mean, dangerous streets. An increasingly uncaring and anonymous reality surrounds the individual while the message is being repeated over and over again to convince him of his need to possess and enjoy everything. The paradoxical nature of modern society is demonstrated by what happens to traffic in sprawling urban areas: they do not all suffer from traffic jams to the same degree, but from Paris to Rome, from Madrid to Tokyo, countless hours are lost, adding up to a huge waste of time and a psychological strain which over a period can gradually become traumatic. These problems show

the absurdities that can result from a booming property market in city centers: city workers can no longer afford to live near their workplaces and once they have been forced out to the suburbs, the marketing sector of the car manufacturing industry then tells them they will need a car — a self-fulfilling prophecy, since unsatisfactory public transport is both caused by, and is a cause of, high levels of car ownership. For the workers themselves, it is a simple fact that a car is a necessity it they are going to be able to reach their offices etc., back in that expensive city center.

But come nightfall, these city centers are deserted; they are often ringed round by derelict urban areas (as in many American cities) inhabited by a large, overcrowded population of those who are poor and "at risk." Arguably, these are the consequences of the practical application of the logic of the market place and of the disintegration of traditonal cultures and their values; they in turn can lead to violence.

This violence is often perpetrated by gangs of young people who roam the streets, left entirely to their own devices in the urban jungle. They exist in gaps between social structures which are becoming ever wider; they have been cut loose from any family infrastructure; they are drifters. Addicted to drugs, (the United States issued an official statement in 1989 identifying drugs as the greatest peril facing the nation) they fight each other in savage urban wars which take a yearly toll of hundreds of dead. This is the picture in Los Angeles and Washington. Large European cities are now also starting to suffer from depredations of such gangs who prey on other young people through extortion, indulge in gang rapes, and commit many other crimes.

The Third World also faces seemingly insuperable problems, particularly in the big cities; this also applies to very large population centers in several South American countries such as Rio de Janeiro, Mexico City, etc. Little progress has been made toward a worldwide social balance.

In part this was due to some regions and

continents being considerably less developed than others; this is still the case and in many instances the gap is growing wider.

Another cause, however, is the fact that our society is becoming more and more urban and yet no truly urban society has been created to cope with the millions of men and women packed into close proximity together in an artificial space. An increasingly complex organization is vital if society is to continue to function; so is respect for a certain number of rules. This means that a conflict of interests now exists between the freedom of the marketplace and the demands of urban management. If we cannot count on the latter, it is not only the city's survival which is threatened but the natural environment as well for these anarchic towns and cities are responsible for a gigantic amount of pollution. At the end of the twentieth century, our society finds itself at a historic crossroads. Posters, by reducing everything to the simplest form of expression, play the role of a magnifying mirror, reflecting the century and its contradictions.

The Development of Poster Art

by Carlo Arturo Quintavalle

The Origins, from Chéret to Toulouse-Lautrec

The development of the poster can be examined in terms of masterpieces created by renowned artists; or—and this approach is more relevant to our times—it can be examined in terms of the artistic problems presented by two characteristics peculiar to posters: the marriage of image and word, and the possibility of duplicating a given poster an infinite number of times. Mass production involved changing one's attitude toward the value of the original print and even minimized the importance of differences between one copy and another. Only later, with the advent of poster collectors, did a more traditional market for posters develop; first proofs then were treated much like paintings, engravings, lithographs, and silk-screen prints. But to understand poster art, we must consider its original function and examine the effect posters had on those for whom they were created.

As with a linguistic system, it is customary to seek the origins of every so-called new art. It goes without saying that one can find antecedents for every phenomenon in almost any era; yet there is not much point in seeking the antecedents of the poster in the heraldic banners or processional flags of ancient Egypt or the civilization of Pompeii. More relevant to its development are the notices and proclamations that began to appear on public walls after the invention of printing. The coming of age of the modern poster is linked to a certain moment in European culture: the transformation of the role of image and word that took place in the second half of the nineteenth century. By that time the industrial revolution had begun to create a consumer economy, and the role of posters came to be to sell, to persuade. By then, too, the development of more sophisticated printing equipment had made mass reproduction feasible. The poster had its first flowering toward the end of that century, in the twin trends of the nar-

Opposite: lithograph by Édouard Manet entitled *The Cats*, 1868; 50 inches by 35 inches. Paris, Bibliothèque Nationale.

Top left: lithograph by Jules Chéret for the *Palais de Glace*, 1896; 49 inches by 35 inches. Paris, Musée des Arts Décoratifs.

Top right: lithograph by Jules Chéret for a carnival production at the Théâtre de l'Opéra, 1896; 48⅝ inches by 34¼ inches. Paris, Musée des Arts Décoratifs.

rative poster made in France by everyone from Jules Chéret to Henri de Toulouse-Lautrec, and the symbolic art nouveau poster prevalent in England, Austria, and Germany.

One ought to begin the history of the modern poster by noting a few early antecedents, which were printed in very small editions for a precise purpose and a limited audience. One of these is Les Chats, created by Édouard Manet in 1868; it was the first poster for the J. Rothschild publishing house. The center illustration from this poster is the only one usually shown, although the complete poster has a text advertising a book about cats with illustrations by Eugène Delacroix, Brueghel, Eugène Viollet-le-Duc, and others. While Les Chats has been called a poster—primarily by historians who wished to place the illustrious Manet among the originators of posters—it does not demonstrate the new rapport between image and word that one might call the key in defining a poster. The image here simply illustrates the title of the book and in fact plays a role secondary to the words.

Much more interesting from the point of view of the history of the poster is Joseph W. Morsen's Five Celebrated Clowns (1856), a wood engraving. In this case not only are the words secondary, they are almost redundant. This engraving and wall placards like it are of no small importance in tracing the development of images on posters, and they are much more significant than the book jackets that some writers have linked to the history of the poster. (By the time of another gigantic circus poster, one for the Sarasani Circus [1897], the image has entirely taken over from the text.)

If we compare the enduring traditions of the theatrical poster with posters inspired by book illustrations—Frederick Walker's design for The Woman in White, for example —the difference in impact of the two strains becomes apparent. True, in Walker's poster —executed by artist William Hooper—the image assumes new importance. The bold woodcut of the woman—which in style was 240 directly related to the representational tra-

Center left: lithograph by Pierre Bonnard for the magazine *La Revue Blanche*, 1894; 35¾ inches by 24 inches. Paris, Musée des Arts Décoratifs.

Center right: lithograph by Henri de Toulouse-Lautrec for Le Divan Japonais, a nightclub, 1895; 30½ inches by 23¼ inches. Paris, Musée des Arts Décoratifs.

Bottom left: lithograph by Henri de Toulouse-Lautrec advertising Victor Joze's book *Reine de Joie*, 1892; 55¾ inches by 37¾ inches. Paris, Musée des Arts Décoratifs.

Bottom right: lithograph by Henri de Toulouse-Lautrec for an appearance by Jane Avril, 1898; 49½ inches by 36 inches. Paris, Musée des Arts Décoratifs.

Top left: lithograph by Henri de Toulouse-Lautrec for an appearance by Jane Avril, 1899; 22 inches by 14 inches. Paris, Musée des Arts Décoratifs.

Top right: lithograph by Pierre Bonnard for a brand of champagne, 1891; 30¾ inches by 23½ inches. Paris, Musée des Arts Décoratifs.

Center left: lithograph by Théophile Alexandre Steinlen for a theater production, 1896; 54½ inches by 38½ inches. Paris, Musée des Arts Décoratifs.

Center right: lithograph by Pierre Bonnard for an art exhibition, 1896; 23 inches by 15 inches. Paris, Musée des Arts Décoratifs.

Bottom left: lithograph by Théophile Alexandre Steinlen for Comiot motorcycles, 1899; 78 inches by 54½ inches. Paris, Musée des Arts Décoratifs.

Bottom right: lithograph by Théophile Alexandre Steinlen for a brand of sterilized milk, 1897; 54¾ inches by 39½ inches. Paris, Musée des Arts Décoratifs.

dition of the pre-Raphaelites (the poster is usually compared to Edward Burne-Jones's *Night*)—dominates the poster. However, the inscription is entirely unrelated to the image. This illustration is obviously directed to quite a different audience from the one being appealed to by the circus posters cited above.

In fact, the origin of the pictorial poster is to be found both in a new function of illustration and in the emergence of a new kind of audience. Poster illustrations derived from the kind displayed outside theaters, whose public was composed of the middle and lower-middle classes, which flocked to the boulevard theaters of Paris.

In France during the last quarter—and above all the last decade—of the nineteenth century, Toulouse-Lautrec, Chéret, and their followers created a revolution. Jules Chéret (1836–1932) drew his posters directly onto the lithographic stone, concentrated on theater posters, and invented a unique style by relating text to image in an entirely new way. He was certainly inspired at the outset by the tradition of the circus poster, but in his posters the words and the illustration are of parallel importance and are inextricably related. Indeed, in time he came to make the words themselves into illustrations.

Already in *Faust* (1869) his baroque roots are evident, and there are reminiscences of Giambattista, and also, I would say, of Giandomenico, Tiepolo, and even Watteau. Chéret's originality was not in his cultural inspiration, which in the civilized France of Honoré Daumier's caricatures was hardly novel; but rather in his presentation. In *Faust* and others of Chéret's early posters, the presentation is substantially academic, with strong colors, bold lines, and foreshortened figures in the foreground, and the background simply sketched in. This is also true of *Les Girard* (1879), although the originality of that poster lies in the distortion of the type and its intricate relation to the image.

Later Chéret's academic manner became infused with much-altered motifs from Toulouse-Lautrec. However, Chéret was

241

Bottom left: lithograph by Frances and Margaret Macdonald and Herbert McNair, 1894; 88 inches by 35 inches. Milan, Bertarelli Collection.

Bottom right: lithograph by Alphonse Marie Mucha, 1897; 70¼ inches by 24 inches. Paris, Musée des Arts Décoratifs.

Above: lithograph by J. and W. Beggarstaff (pseudonym for William Nicholson and James Pryde), 1897; 76 inches by 77½ inches. Paris, Musée des Arts Décoratifs.

Left: lithograph by Aubrey Beardsley, 1894; 29 inches by 19 inches. New York, Museum of Modern Art.

never as original as Toulouse-Lautrec, because he never abandoned his experiments with the style of the Italian baroque and of French rococo prints.

The artistic inspiration of Henri de Toulouse-Lautrec (1864–1901) was completely different. In place of academicism, he had a profound knowledge of Japanese wood engraving; in place of the rococo he was influenced by the postimpressionists and above all by Vincent van Gogh and Paul Gauguin at his most "oriental." With this background Toulouse-Lautrec drew not generic figures but individual faces. He invented a way to combine words and images so that the images took on a narrative function and the words accompanied the images without overpowering them as they tended to do in Chéret's posters.

In the poster Reine de Joie *(1892), Toulouse-Lautrec's characteristic flat colors and foreshortening are already present; but the inscription, simply superimposed on the illustration and somewhat muted by its flat green color, has not yet become an illustration itself, nor has it assumed equal importance with the image, as it would a little later. On the other hand Toulouse-Lautrec has already abandoned academic conventions: he has barely sketched the surroundings, the plates, and the vaguely art nouveau jug. Only the woman is painted in vibrant colors. Toulouse-Lautrec treated the inscription in the same way two years later in a well-known poster he did for another of Victor Joze's novels,* Babylone d'Allemagne. *By contrast, in the same year, 1894, Pierre Bonnard designed for* La Revue Blanche *one of the most important posters, in which the words are very much a part of the design for the illustration: each brick in the back-*

ground is inscribed with the name of the magazine.

Toulouse-Lautrec also did posters for La Revue Blanche, notably one in 1895, the same year he did one for the nightclub Divan Japonais. Among the innovations in the latter are the woman in black looming in the foreground and the cellos of the orchestra in grainy gray in the background. The woman's face is an example of Toulouse-Lautrec's violent and vivid portrait technique, which we see again in the series Jane Avril. In the Jane Avril of 1898 even the cello recurs.

Toulouse-Lautrec's poster illustrations are metaphors composed of allusive, emblematic details. The words that fill the "voids" between the images serve only to clarify them. In this sense another poster in the Jane Avril series, executed in 1899, seems to me most interesting. It bears only the words "Jane Avril." No longer are there allusions to the orchestra, the stage set, the public, and the musical score as in so many other posters. This poster states only the essential and thus makes one think of certain Gauguins that by this time Toulouse-Lautrec must have known.

Toulouse-Lautrec's genius is diverse, not because he was an "artist" but because he invented a synthetic, revolutionary means of telling a story that was much more advanced than that being proposed in contemporary painting. It was truly understood, in my opinion, only by the English artists William Nicholson (1872–1949) and James Pryde (1866–1941), who signed their posters "J. and W. Beggarstaff." It was certainly not understood in France or in cultures influenced by that of France.

Except for the one he did for La Revue Blanche, Bonnard's posters are rather ordinary. In France Champagne (1891), for example, and Salon des Cent (1896), the approach to words is regressive compared to Toulouse-Lautrec's. Painters in general have not been terribly important to the history of posters, but I would like to mention Félix Vallotton for his poster La Pépinière, done before 1894; Maurice

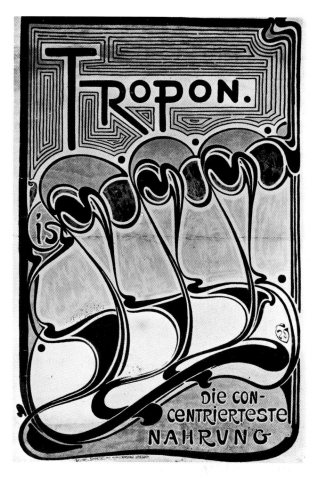

Henry Van de Velde, *Tropon, die concentrierste Nahrung*, 1889. Lithograph; Paris, Musée des Arts Décoratifs.

Top left: lithograph by Oskar Kokoschka for a series of summer theater productions, 1907; 46½ inches by 30 inches. Private collection.

Top right: lithograph by Egon Schiele for a series of lectures, 1910; 24¾ inches by 14½ inches. Private collection.

Denis' La Dépêche de Toulouse *(1895), which is obviously influenced by the symbolists; Jacques Villon and his* Maggie Berck *(1904), and finally Théophile Alexandre Steinlen (1859–1923).*

Steinlen is the link between the tradition of Chéret and Toulouse-Lautrec, which he synthesized in a clumsy fashion, and the subsequent tradition of the poster in France. But he remained outside the art nouveau style, which was developing in the rest of Europe, and therefore also outside the tradition of the Bauhaus. Steinlen's Tournée du Chat Noir *(1896), with its emblematic cat in the immediate foreground, shows the artist's debt to Toulouse-Lautrec. It also shows how he transformed elements characteristic of Toulouse-Lautrec into a tiresome, descriptive poster. Most of his posters advertised products for sale rather than theatrical performances.*

Steinlen developed very much of a storytelling format for his posters, as in the one for Comiot motorbikes (1899) and the one for sterilized milk (1897). In the latter the words are simply headlines, and the illustration is minutely detailed in the most banal graphic tradition. The great "cultural" moment of the French poster was over, although an echo of it, brilliantly reinvented, is to be found in the work of J. and W. Beggarstaff. The tradition in which they worked, it seems to me, evokes Toulouse-Lautrec's first rather Japanese moments and returns to the roots of impressionism and—more recently—of symbolism.

The Art Nouveau Tradition in Europe

The style variously called liberty, art nouveau, and Jugendstil was a phenomenon that emerged across Europe. It led to a substantial change in the relationship of words and images in posters, and except in France

it dominated the culture of Europe for fifteen years, spanning the turn of the century. The principal representatives of the style in Europe were William Morris (1834–96) and Aubrey Beardsley (1872–98) in England, Margaret (1865–1933) and Frances (1874–1921) Macdonald and Charles Rennie Mackintosh (1868–1928) in Scotland, the Czechoslovakian-born Alphonse Marie Mucha (1860–1939) in France, Jan Toorop (1858–1928) in Holland, Henry van de Velde (1863–1957) in Belgium, and Gustave Klimt (1862–1918) in Austria. In his influential marginal drawings for Le Roman de Godefroi de Bouillon *(1893), Morris went back to fifteenth-century Flemish manuscript decorations, thereby starting a medieval revival. Among those affected by the Gothic elements of this revival and by its demonic myths were two groups of German*

244

Photomontage by John Heartfield entitled *Ten Years Later: Fathers and Sons*, 1924. Private collection.

Below left: photomontage by John Heartfield entitled *Hurrah, There Is No More Butter!* 1935. Private collection.

Below right: photomontage by John Heartfield entitled *Monuments of Fascist Glory*, 1936. Private collection.

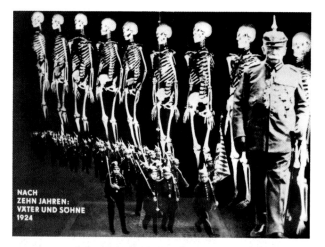

signed posters in the tradition of Chéret, as for example two posters he did for Sarah Bernhardt, one advertising Medée of 1898 and one advertising La Samaritaine (1897). The most inventive contributors to the Jugendstil were Toorop and van de Velde. In Toorop's Delftsche Slaolie *word and illustration* are perfectly integrated. Indeed the descriptive function of the illustration has been transformed. The sinuous, repetitive line weaves a tapestry in which the figures and the liquid being poured on the greens in the bowl become secondary to the total design.

In van de Velde's very famous poster for Tropon (1899) the illustration is ambiguous and allusive, almost as abstract as a trademark, while the inscription is explicit. The Jugendstil is a far cry from the realism of French posters at the end of the nineteenth century.

In the design that Gustave Klimt created for a poster for the first Secession show in Vienna in 1898 and reused to advertise the Austrian art magazine Ver Sacrum in the same year, the illustration showing Theseus killing the minotaur while Minerva looks on is entirely symbolic. The scene even has its own headline on the column at the upper left, which proclaims "Theseus und Minotaurus." The inscription relating to the Ver Sacrum *might as well be part of another poster.* This trend toward posters that exist on two levels simultaneously was not continued between the time of the Jugendstil and the time of the Bauhaus. During the intervening years French realism or German expressionism prevailed in poster art, and posters took off in an entirely different direction.

expressionist artists—Die Brücke, which formed in Dresden and moved in 1911 to Berlin, and Der Blaue Reiter, which was formed in Munich in 1912. The importance of Gothic lettering and its relationship to poster illustration grew even greater.

In his poster for A Comedy of Sighs (1894), among others, Aubrey Beardsley drew on the French narrative tradition. The Japanese style of the words "Avenue Theatre" gives them the value of images. But in the poster for the Glasgow Institute of the Fine Arts by the Macdonalds and Herbert McNair, another point of view in the current debate about the function of words and illustrations is evident. The illustration here does not explain the words; on the contrary, it is a separate symbol.

In the beginning Mucha, by contrast, de-

German Expressionism and the War Poster in the West

The expressionist revolution was influenced by the discovery in the West of Japanese wood engravings, the revival of populist nationalism, the Jugendstil, and a certain civic-mindedness. Expressionism—which was symbolic, emotional, sometimes violent, and always nonrealistic—had a particular impact on film posters, for example the 1919 poster for The Cabinet of Dr. Caligari and the anonymous one for Der Golem (1920). It also greatly affected posters created during and immediately after the First World War, such as Arbeiter, Hunger Tod . . . (1919) by Heinz Fuchs.

The position of Oskar Kokoschka (born in 1886) is complex. His artistic vision was formed during the years of the Jugendstil and was particularly influenced by Klimt (see the lithographs for Die Traumenden Knaben). He was also influenced by Japanese prints and their imitators in France (see Fan on Swan's Skin), and by Gauguin, particularly in his works of 1907 and 1908. While studying in Vienna from 1905 to 1909 Kokoschka thoroughly explored the art exhibition there, particularly admiring the paintings of Edvard Munch and Vincent van Gogh. Kokoschka's varied circle of friends included Gustav Meyrink, the author of symbolic, often grotesque novels such as Der Golem and Walpurgisnacht, who explored the connection between demonic myths and German nationalism. Kokoschka saw the plays of Henrik Ibsen staged, and he knew the work of symbolist writers Frank Wedekind and Carl Sternheim. He loved the popular Bohemian paintings on glass that so interested Vasili Kandinski, a member of the Blaue Reiter. The complexity of Kokoschka's artistic background is evident in his 1907 poster Drama-Komoedie. Egon Schiele's (1890–1918) Shaw oder die Ironie (1910) in turn betrays Kokoschka's influence on him.

But if these are posters for the elite be-

cause of their complexity, expressionism also produced wartime posters of a less concentrated and more accessible nature. One among many German ones is Das ist der Weg zum Frieden, by Lucien Bernhard. Kokoschka's Nieder mit dem Bolschewismus is another.

The wartime poster followed local tradition in other countries. Thus it was realistic in France and in the United States. From the latter came the famous although mediocre I Want You for the U.S. Army, by James Montgomery Flagg and That Liberty Shall Not Perish from the Earth, by Joseph Pennell, which is even worse. The technique of photomontage, which the avant-garde Dadaists were using during the war, was not used in wartime posters, which remained for the most part solidly realistic. The inscriptions, once again quite

Typographic theater poster by Aleksandr Rodchenko entitled *INGA*, about 1920; 29½ inches by 41½ inches. New York, Museum of Modern Art; gift of Jay Leyda.

separate from the illustrations, simply proclaimed slogans.

The Bauhaus

There was a certain continuity between the posters of Toulouse-Lautrec and Steinlen, but between 1920 and 1922 poster art divided into two streams: one for the masses, the other for the elite.

Three principal factors were involved in creating this divergence: the Dadaist movement of 1916 in Zurich and of 1918 in Paris; Russian artist Kazimir Malevich's suprematism (a nonobjective style, in which flat geometric shapes were painted on the bare canvas) and his connection with the origins of the Dutch artists' movement known as De Stijl in 1917; and the first Bauhaus at Weimar in 1919, in which were united the fantastic-mythic inspiration of Paul Klee and Kandinski and the structuralism of architects, poster makers, and other graphic artists. One of the key figures in the culture of this period was the Russian nonobjective artist Eliezer Lissitzky.

During and immediately after the First World War, a period of crisis in poster art, the poster received fresh inspiration from two directions: the photomontage technique practiced by the Dadaists of Berlin, who were active from about 1917 to 1923, and the Bauhaus use of type. The major figures using photomontage were Raoul Hausmann, beginning in 1918, John Heartfield, George Grosz, and Hannah Höch.

Heartfield is the key to an understanding of the development of the Russian poster during the late 1920's and the 1930's. He began by collaborating with Grosz in making collages. Besides posters, he designed striking photomontage book jackets. In his posters there is always a large figure in the foreground that is contrasted with others receding in exaggerated perspective. The posters depend for their effect on the violent contrast between these two elements. The inscription simply underlines an argument already evident in the illustration. Among his famous posters are Adolf, der Übermensch of 1932 and Hurrah, die Butter ist alle! (1935). The latter is an ironic commentary on Hermann Göring's statement: "Bronze has made the Reich strong, butter and lard have made the people flaccid and fat." Another ironic poster is Faschistische Ruhmesmale (1936), in which Mussolini appears as the Sphinx next to a pyramid of skulls.

It is curious how the Dadaist technique of dislocating images, which was intended for an elite when it was first used in Zurich in 1916 and in Paris in 1918, became transformed into a means of educating masses of viewers in political analysis.

Russia was the most fertile ground for the Dadaist poster. After a brief flirtation with the experiments of Lissitzky and sculptor

247

Below left: poster by G. Klutsis celebrating the completion of the first Russian five-year plan in the field of transportation, 1929; 27¼ inches by 19¼ inches. New York, Museum of Modern Art.

Below left: linoleum cut by Walter Dexel for a photography exhibition at Magdeburg, 1929; 33 inches by 23 inches. New York, Museum of Modern Art; gift of the artist.

Above right: lithograph by Joost Schmidt for an exhibition of the Bauhaus at Weimar, 1923; 26¼ inches by 18½ inches. New York, Museum of Modern Art; gift of Walter Gropius.

Above right: offset lithograph by Herbert Bayer for an exhibition of European handicrafts, 1927; 19¼ inches by 12½ inches. New York, Museum of Modern Art; gift of Mr. and Mrs. Alfred H. Barr, Jr.

Vladimir Tatlin and before that with the work of Malevich, the Russians accepted the work that Heartfield was doing in Berlin; and although they mistakenly believed that it was realism, they practiced it at every level from the 1920's until the end of the Second World War. Lissitzky himself became converted to this aesthetic, as one can see by his 1929 poster U.S.S.R. Russische Ausstellung. Another Russian poster of 1929 also demonstrates the trend toward Dadaist photomontage: G. Klutsis' poster for the completion of the first five-year plan in the field of transportation.

From the period before his conversion to photomontage techniques until the end of the 1920's, Lissitzky was an innovator of genius and the link between the Russian avant-garde and the Bauhaus. In Bauhaus posters the inscriptions became illustrations. The unity of words and illustration in Bauhaus work is extremely rich and complex, and by the very structure of Bauhaus production, posters remained for the elite. But in the long run the Bauhaus could not help but influence the development of the poster in Europe, particularly in Switzerland after the Nazis took over in Germany and the poster there returned to an academic, rhetorical realism.

Joost Schmidt's (1893–1942) Staatliches Bauhaus Ausstellung (1923) shows the intimate interaction of the words and the geometric illustration. The type design recalls earlier experiments by Lissitzky and the suprematism of Malevich's paintings. One of the more influential men in the Bauhaus was Walter Dexel (born in 1890), whose Fotografie der Gegenwart (1929) is shown here.

But perhaps the most important man in the Bauhaus so far as posters are concerned was the Austrian Herbert Bayer (born in 1900), whose work can be closely related to that of László Moholy-Nagy and Josef Albers. His Ausstellung Europäisches Kunstgewerbe (1927) is reminiscent of one of Alber's experiments with the alphabet entitled Entwürfe zur Schablonenschrift (1925) and Bayer's own earlier 3 Vorstudien für das Universalalfabet. Among those who united photomontage and graphic design were Jan Tschichold (born in Leipzig in 1902), Alfred Mahlau (born in Berlin in 1894, died in Hamburg in 1967), Kandinski (in his Jubiläums-Ausstellung of 1926), and Piet Zwart (born in Holland in 1885).

Purely geometric are the posters of the German C. O. Muller (born in 1893) and the early works of the Russian Aleksandr

248

Rodchenko (whose later realistic style can be seen in INGA, a theater poster probably of the early 1920's).

From the Postcubist Poster to the Second World War

In the 1930's European posters reflected several trends: the postcubist synthesis; simplified and depoliticized versions of the photomontages of the Berlin Dadaists; and the Dadaists' borrowings from surrealism.

Adolphe Mouron Cassandre (born in Cracow in 1901) created a real alternative to the Russian photomontage poster and the Bauhaus poster. One of his first and most important posters was Nord Express, done for the French railroads in 1927. The train—foreshortened in a futurist fashion—and the overhead electric wires suggest great speed. The words, however, are simply captions, as though the Bauhaus had never existed.

Among the most interesting poster artists of the postcubist revival was the American E. McKnight-Kauffer (1890–1954), whose poster for the film Metropolis owes an obvious debt to Lissitzky. He developed a rather stylized realism in Power, the Nerve Centre of London's Underground, and then abandoned that for the calculated visual ambiguity of Magicians Prefer Shell. Later, in 1924, the Frenchman Jean Carlu (born in 1900) took up cubist themes again in America's Answer, Production.

Some poster artists of the 1930's followed noncubist leads, among them Herbert Matter (born in 1907 in Switzerland). He united the photomontage techniques of Heartfield with a minutely detailed interpretation of reality—surrealism, in short.

The wartime posters of Germany and Italy, addressed to the masses and necessarily rather rhetorical, are less interesting than those created in other countries. In the United States, for example, the artist Ben Shahn made many posters, among them Years of Dust and This Is Nazi Brutality Leo Lionni's Keep 'Em Rolling (1941),

another American wartime poster, is a good example of contemporary photomontage. Dadaist elements are evident in Your Talk May Kill Your Comrades by the Englishman Abram Games.

Postwar Tendencies

It may appear easier to follow the development of the poster in recent times, but in fact the poster today has acquired a much greater importance and a much more complex character than it had in the past. Earlier it was possible to single out the middle European poster, or the Russian poster, or the French poster after Chéret, and so on, but now national and cultural distinctions can no longer be made.

In the West, except for appeals for blood or campaigns against cancer, tuberculosis, or pollution, public service posters have almost entirely been replaced by publicity posters. Within the category of publicity posters, one must distinguish the metaphorical ones from the more literal ones used to advertise films. The latter preserve the poster at the level of pure and detailed illustration.

249

Above: tempera poster by E. McKnight-Kauffer for the film *Metropolis*, 1926; 18½ inches by 30 inches. New York, Museum of Modern Art.

In Eastern Europe, on the other hand, because of the different economic system,
there is a prevalence of posters announcing
cultural events from plays to art films, promoting civic events, and drawing public attention to community projects. In Russia the
photomontage poster today is often full of
rhetorical clichés.

Among the phenomena of the Western
poster is a group created by artists famous
for their work in other genres. This development began at the end of the 1940's, grew
rapidly during the 1950's and 1960's, and
only now is beginning to diminish in significance. Among the artists involved are
Pablo Picasso, Joan Miró, Georges Braque,
Fernand Léger, Henri Matisse, Max Ernst,
Salvador Dali, and Max Bill. For the most
part their posters are nothing more or less
than reproductions of a detail or other element from a larger picture. They do not pre-
tend to be accessible to all viewers but simply to be a kind of monogram that only the
initiated will understand. These posters are
very often included in catalogues and studies of the history of the poster, but in fact
they are of very little importance in the development of mass culture.

Therefore I will analyze only a few examples of the genre, limiting myself to those
posters that present substantial pictorial
innovations. The work of the Frenchman
Raymond Savignac (born in 1907) combines
realism with caricature, but it is not particularly innovative. Linked to the Bauhaus
(which is still the richest source of novelties
for modern graphic artists) is the poster
work of the Italian artist Giovanni Pintori
(born in 1912), the work of Leo Lionni, and
that of the American Tomoko Miho (born in
1931). Among the modern makers of photomontage posters, often clearly inspired by
Heartfield, are two Swiss artists, Hans Erni
(born in 1909) and Carlo Vivarelli (born in
1919). Surrealist motifs are characteristic
of the work of the Swiss Herbert Leupin
(born in 1916). Constructivism is reflected in
the posters of the Swiss Max Bill (born in
1908) and of the German Wolfgang Schmidt
(born in 1930).

Painter Roy Lichtenstein's technique of using multiple images has also been employed in advertising posters, sometimes most effectively, as in Campari, by the Italian Bruno Munari (born in 1907). Other poster artists who have used this technique are the Englishmen Eduardo Paolozzi (born in 1924) and Peter Gee (born in 1932), the Brazilian Almin Mavignier (born in 1926), the Mexican Eduardo Terrazas (born in 1936), the American Lance Wyman (born in 1937), and the German Johannes Reyn. I could go on, but I prefer to mention a few of the really modern posters created by painters, rather than those in the old tradition of gallery posters done by such men as Picasso and Miró. Among these truly modern posters are the Paris Review posters by Escobar Marisol and Andy Warhol, and certain posters by Frank Stella, Lichtenstein, and Robert Indiana.

In conclusion I would like to note that the realistic poster continues to decline, while the new, metaphorical publicity poster is increasingly in evidence. In the latter the written words themselves become illustrations.

Offset lithograph by Bruno Munari, 1965; 77½ inches by 109 inches. New York, Museum of Modern Art; gift of the artist.

Below: offset lithograph by Eduardo Terrazas and Lance Wyman for the 1968 Olympics, 1967; 35 inches by 34 inches. New York, Museum of Modern Art; gift of the Committee for the 19th Olympics.

A poster should never be thought of as a painting; it should be considered only in the context of the specific publicity campaign to which it belongs. Among other things, a publicity poster on a wall is a reduced image of a more complex advertising message that establishes a dialogue with the viewer. Because of this, a history of posters abstracted from their social context and the specific advertising campaigns in which they figured would be both incomplete and misleading.

I would suggest, therefore, that to trace the development of postwar posters, one should try to reconstruct the context in which they appeared. Only by considering them as part of their respective publicity campaigns, rather than as the work of individual artists, can a historically accurate appraisal of them be made.

Below: silk-screen print by Andy Warhol for the *Paris Review*, 1967; 37 inches by 27 inches. New York, Museum of Modern Art; gift of Page, Arbitrio and Rese.

Silk-screen print by Marisol for the *Paris Review*, 1967; 32 inches by 34 inches. New York, Museum of Modern Art; gift of Page, Arbitrio and Rese.

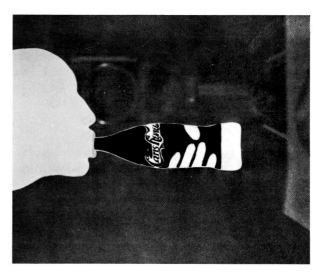

The poster: from political message to collector's item

From 1970 onward the importance of the poster and its communicative role in society appears to have radically changed in contrast to the 1950's and and 1960's, when posters — both advertising and political ones — used to occupy a central position in the field of communication. Television, for example, has overtaken the poster in this way, posters these days tending to echo advertisements initially broadcast on television or published in magazines.

Together with this shift in emphasis in favor of the other media, there has been a change throughout the world in the way posters are used. In the 1960's Castro's Cuba was a focal point in the development of pop culture in the United States, and in the 1970's Allende's Chile and the political situation in Mexico and Vietnam captured the popular imagination, but now most of these poster images have lost their visual impact. If we look at pictures of the anti-Khomeini struggle (together with previous anti-Shah ones by Khomeini supporters), and posters from African countries condemning apartheid, colonialism, or stressing economic difficulties, the poster as it is used in this sense fulfills an educative

Above: Brittner, West Germany, 1986. "Wasser." The symbols are reversed: here the umbrella protects the rain from man. Anti-pollution environmentalist poster.

Alain Le Quernec, France, 1982. The poster tells a story to be quoted: here a tear and a Solidarity badge are added to the famous image of Lenin, in the wake of the coup in Poland.

253

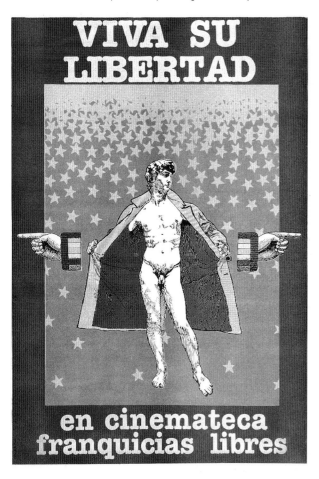

purpose in the absence of other means of communication, a function it no longer has in other areas.

In the Western world posters are no longer as relevant as they used to be because they have become desirable collector's items. In New York and every other major city in the industrialized world, posters — now already historical — of Che Guevara of the student revolution of May 1968, of the PLO or Stalinist in their message, sell alongside Mickey Mouse faces, pictures of Coke bottles, Sting or Madonna. The poster has been elevated to the realms of mythological image.

With the postwar triumph of the Bauhaus a neo-rationalist image came to the fore and prevailed up to the 1960's, except in the Eastern bloc countries where realism continued to dominate. Finally, the pop revolution overturned the old principles and trends. In the 1970's another radical revolution in language took place, borrowing elements from Dada and Surrealism, Pop and Futurism, leading to the discovery of color, child-like writing, sprays and graffiti. In this sense posters in the West may be seen as experiment-

ing with a new language that is inevitably addressed to an elitist audience. Posters and periodicals published in Paris, Berlin, Munich, and London between 1968 and 1977 bear witness to this.

The most striking contrasts in poster art in the West are to be found in the field of advertising. Compare, for instance, advertisements for beverages in recent years and similar ones produced around 1970. Today the only language that is acceptable to the public is a complex one: the poster is no longer a straightforward narrative, but a series of hints to a public familiar with the language of advertising and able to interpret its symbols and messages. The poster uses a sophisticated language to trigger this interpretative process.

Posters are therefore changing. Poster shops will eventually proliferate in every small town, and more people will begin to collect last year's advertisement posters; the transformation, which has only recently begun, of the poster's role in our culture will then be made manifest, and its transition from an instrument of political persuasion to a collectable item complete.

Bibliography

Adhémar, J. *Cent ans d'affiches dans le monde* (exhibition). Paris: Bibliothèque Nationale, 1972.

Amstutz, W. *Who's Who in Graphic Art.* Zurich: Amstutz and Herdeg Graphic Press, 1962.

Bilbo, J. *Toulouse-Lautrec and Steinlen.* London: 1946.

Boudet, M. G. *Les affiches étrangères.* Paris: 1898.

Breitenbach, E. *The Poster Craze.* New York: *American Heritage Magazine,* 1962.

Constantin, M., and Ferm, A. M. *World and Image* (exhibition). New York: The Museum of Modern Art, 1968.

Contini, M. *La donna nel manifesto* (exhibition). Arezzo: Castello di Poppi, 1970.

Frenzel, H. K. *Ludwig Hohlwein und sein Werk.* Berlin: 1938.

Hampel, J., and Grulich, R. *Politische Plakate der Gegenwart.* Munich: Bruckmann, 1971.

Hardie, M. *War Poster: 1914–1918.* London: 1920.

Herzfelde, W. *John Heartfield.* Dresden: VEB Verlag der Kunst, 1971.

Hillier, B. *Histoire de l'Affiche.* Paris: Librairie Fayard, 1969–70.

Hutchison, H. F. *The Poster: An Illustrated History from 1860.* New York: The Viking Press, 1969.

Koch, R. *Art Nouveau Posters.* Paris: Gazette des Beaux Arts, 1969–70.

McKnight-Kauffer, E. *The Art of the Poster.* London: 1924.

Maindron, E. *Les affiches illustrées: 1866.* Paris: 1867.

——— *Les affiches illustrées: 1886–1895.* Paris, 1896.

Price, C. Matlock. *Poster Designers.* New York: 1922.

Purvis, T. *Poster Progress.* London: 1940.

Rademacher, H. *Arte del Manifesto in Germania: 1896–1933.* Milan: La Pietra, 1965.

Reade, B. *Art Nouveau and Alphonse Mucha.* London: Victoria and Albert Museum, 1967.

——— *Aubrey Beardsley* (exhibition). London: Victoria and Albert Museum, 1967.

Rickards, M. *L'Affiche Anglaise: les années 90* (exhibition). Paris, Musée des Arts Décoratifs, 1972.

——— *Banned Posters.* London: Evelyn, Adams & Mackay Ltd., 1969.

——— *Internationale Plakate: 1871–1971* (exhibition). Munich: Haus der Kunst, 1971–72.

——— Manifesti francesi del 19° secolo (exhibition). Milan: Centro Rizzoli, 1970.

——— *1920's Posters.* London: Evelyn, Adams & Mackay Ltd., 1968.

——— *Posters of the First World War.* London: Evelyn, Adams & Mackay Ltd., 1968.

——— *Posters of Protest and Revolution.* Bath: Somerset, Adams & Dart, 1970.

——— *Posters at the Turn of the Century.* London: Evelyn, Adams & Mackay Ltd., 1968.

——— *The Rise and Fall of the Poster.* Newton Abbot, Devon, David & Charles, 1971.

——— *Vienna Secession: Art Nouveau to 1970* (exhibition). London: Royal Academy of Arts, 1971.

Rogers, W. S. *A Book of the Poster.* London: 1901.

Rossi, A. *I manifesti.* Milan: Fratelli Fabbri Editori, 1966.

Rotzler, W. *Meister der Plakatkunst* (exhibition). Zurich: Kunstgewerbemuseum, 1959.

Salanon, R. *Cent ans d'affiches: "La Belle Époque"* (exhibition). Paris: Musée des Arts Decoratifs, 1964.

Sangiorgi, G., Mascherpa, G., and Veronesi, G. *Grafica Ricordi, dal manifesto storico alla produzione d'avanguardia* (exhibition). Rome: Ente Premi, 1967.

Sponsel, J. L. *Das Moderne Plakat.* Dresden: 1897.

Veronesi, G. *L'Opera Lirica nell'Avviso Teatrale* (exhibition). Milan: Museo Teatrale alla Scala, 1966.

Villani, D. *La Belle Époque dei gionali Italiani nel manifesto* (exhibition). Milan: Comune di Milano, 1969.

Wember, P. *Die Jugend der Plakate: 1887–1917.* Krefeld: Scherpe Verlag, 1962.

White, G. *The Poster and Its Artistic Possibilities.* London: 1896.

Picture Credits

Paul Bytebier, Brussels, for the Musée de l'Armée et d'Histoire Militaire
Sally Chapper, Richmond, for the Victoria and Albert Museum
Pino Dal Gal, Verona, for pages 215, 281, 287, 289, and 290
Carlo Dani, Milan, for the Museo del Risorgimento
G. Fini, Treviso, for the Museo Civico Luigi Bailo, Salce Collection
Giraudon, Paris, for page 15
Heinz Müller, Stuttgart, for the Staatsgalerie
F. Kimmel, Paris, for the black and white art from the Musée des Arts Décoratifs
R. Lalance, Paris, for the color art from the Musée des Arts Décoratifs
La Photothèque Française, Paris, for the Musée de la Guerre
Lotte Esser, Darmstadt, for the Hessisches Landesmuseum
Agenzia Novosti, Rome, for pages 209 (2), 210, 212, 240 (1), and 261
Christine Sheppard, London, for the London Museum
Agenzia S.I.P.R.A., Turin, for page 49
Agence Snark, Paris, for pages 191, 204(1)
Foto Tabti, Meudon la Forêt, for pages 220 (left), 224 (right), 229, 231, 253 (left), 254 (left)
Union des Arts Décoratifs, Paris, for pages 218, 219, 221 223 (above), 224 (left), 227 (below), 232–3, 234, 235 (below), 236, 253
Société des Amis de la Bibliothèque Forney, Paris, for pages 220 (right), 222, 223 (below), 225, 226, 227 (above), 228, 230 254 (right)

© S.P.A.D.E.M.: Adrien Barrère; Pierre Bonnard; Jules Chéret; Paul Colin; Oskar Kokoschka; Christian Massias; Théophile Steinlen; Félix Vallotton

© A.D.A.G.P.: G. Capon,; Jean Carlu; A. M. Cassandre; Man Ray; Orazi

The illustrations from collections and museums not cited above were furnished by the photography departments of the collections and museums cited in the caption credits.

The Editors would particularly like to thank the Agenzia di Stampa Novosti; the Embassy of the Netherlands in Rome; the Food and Agriculture Organization of the United Nations; Maria Constantin Severini, Paris; Mary Franco Lao, Rome; Belinda Loftus of the Imperial War Museum, London; Luigi Menegazzi of the Museo Civico Luigi Bailo, Treviso; Ch. Pérassaux of the Bibliothèque Nationale, Paris; Géneviève Picon of the Bibliothèque des Arts Décoratifs, Paris, and her colleagues Anne Kimmel and Dominique Negel; Bob Schwartz, New York; Maria Teresa Berti, Paris; Sarah Cobb, London; Lisa Goldberg, New York; and Graziella Passera, Munich.